BROWNSEA

DORSET'S FANTASY ISLAND

Rodney Legg

dpc
DORSET PUBLISHING COMPANY
Knock-na-cre, Milborne Port, Sherborne, Dorset DT9 5HJ

Also by Rodney Legg

Purbeck Island
A Guide to Dorset Ghosts
Ghosts of Dorset, Devon and Somerset
Editor *Steep Holm – a case history in the study of ecology*
Annotator *Monumenta Britannica* with John Fowles
Exploring Ancient Wiltshire with George Osborn
Old Portland with Jean M Edwards
Romans in Britain
Purbeck Walks
Old Swanage
The Dorset Walk with Ron Dacombe, Colin Graham
Stonehenge Antiquaries
Guide to Purbeck Coast and Shipwreck
Hardy Country Walks
The Steep Holm Guide
Lulworth and Tyneham Revisited
Walks in West Dorset
The Blandford Forum Guide
National Trust Dorset with Colin Graham
Dorset's War 1939-45
Cerne's Giant and Village Guide
Purbeck's Heath – claypits, nature and the oilfield
East Dorset Country Walks
Blackmore Vale and Cranborne Chase Walks
Exploring the Heartland of Purbeck

To Jo Shrimpton
from a different island

Publishing details. First published 1986.
Text copyright Rodney Legg © 1986.
Restriction upon copying. All rights reserved. No part of this publication may be reproduced, stored in a retrieval system, or transmitted in any form or by any means, electronic, recorded, photocopied or otherwise, without prior permission in writing from the copyright owner.
Printing credits. Typeset by Jackie Sugg at Typestyle, The Lynx Trading Estate, Yeovil, Somerset and by Irene Howard at SOS Typesetting, Bell Street, Shaftesbury, Dorset. Printed in Great Britain by Wincanton Litho, Wincanton, Somerset, with platemaking by Andrew Johnstone and machining by Steve Taylor. Bound at Castle Cary Press, Somerset.
Distribution. Trade sales distribution by Dorset Publishing Company from Knock-na-cre, Milborne Port, Sherborne, Dorset DT9 5HJ, telephone 0963 32583 or 0963 33643.
International standard book number (ISBN) 0 902129 74 0

IMPORTANT PUBLIC ACCESS INFORMATION

Brownsea Island lies in the middle of Dorset's Poole Harbour. It covers 500 acres and is owned by the National Trust. The island is generally open to the public from about the start of April to the end of September and is served by ferries from Poole Quay and Sandbanks. Visitors with their own boats may land at Pottery Pier at the west end of the island. The Trust has asked us to point out that in periods of prolonged drought the island may have to be closed because of the fire risk. The Trust feels we should also stress that there is no public access to two of the principal features described in the book. The Castle is leased as a private hotel, for the workers of the John Lewis Partnership, and most of the northern part of the island is a nature reserve established by the Dorset Naturalists' Trust [re-named the Dorset Trust for Nature Conservation in 1986]. This reserve has limited controlled access, with guided tours. There is a third restricted area on the central southern shore, which because of its historical assocations is used for scout and guide camps, and some smaller parts of the island are reserved for wardening purposes. The author's thanks must be extended to Alan Bromby, Brownsea's head warden, who took photographer Colin Graham out in his boat and accepted the burden of reading the proofs. As an island warden myself, of something much smaller and rockier – Steep Holm in the Bristol Channel – I feel a rapport with Alan. I was relieved therefore that he expressed 'Congratulations on the book.' I realise I might be less charitable towards someone who presumed to chart my territory.

BROWNSEA IS a fantasy island; our legacy from wealthy, charismatic eccentrics. Few places have a stronger history. The agreeable bonus is that a ferry ride from Poole Quay or Sandbanks puts a different world at your feet. The island today is a treasure of the National Trust and Dorset Naturalists' Trust which in high summer is a paradise of Mediterranean warmth with an exotic vegetation of strawberry trees and other parkland escapes along its southern shore. The shallow harbour waters give it a mild microclimate. Brownsea is the largest island in Poole Harbour, having a length of well over a mile and 496 acres above the high-tide mark.

The name: Brunksay, Branksea to Brownsea

Brownsea appears in the Domesday survey of 1086 as *Brunci's Insula* [Bruno's Island] and in mediaeval documents the corruptions proliferate. It is *Brunksey, Brunkesay* and *Brunsey,* to pick the main-stream versions. The island was then part of the manor of Stollant [Studland] and indeed it is still in that Purbeck civil parish. The closest mainland quay, in the Middle Ages, was not Poole but Redhorn – now totally deserted – on the western side of the South Haven Peninsula.

Brunksey gradually became *Branksea.* By the nineteenth century *Brownsea* had made its debut but to Poole people it was *Branksea,* which name was still on its boat into the 1930s and was in general use by elderly people in Poole into the 1980s. Charles van Raalte was the culprit, at the turn of the century, for Brownsea's ascendancy, though he had a compelling and practical reason which I'll give later in the story.

1880s

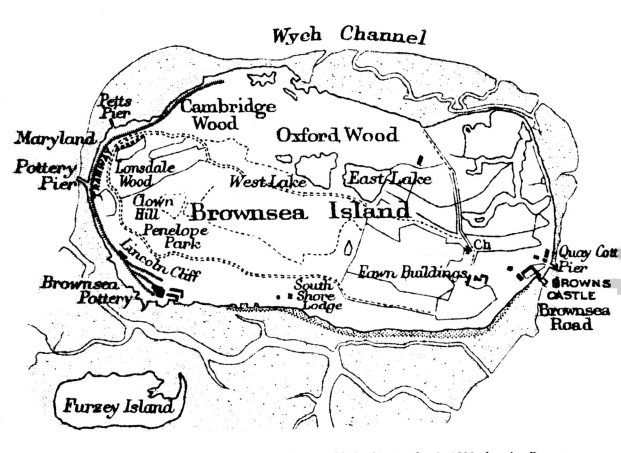

Map by F. S. Weller and W. H. Everett and Son, published in London in 1890, showing Brownsea Island at the close of industrial activity. There is a tramway from the claypits beside the north shore to the Brownsea Pottery at the corner of the island overlooking Furzey Island. There is a misprint – 'Fawn' Buildings, in the south-east quarter, should read 'Farm' Buildings. 'Wych' is now generally spelt 'Wytch' and shows the channel that curves through the central waters of Poole Harbour to Shipstal Point at Arne and then narrows for its final southwards turn to Wytch Passage beside the twentieth century oil-field on the Rempstone Estate in the Isle of Purbeck.
Source: Rodney Legg collection

Iron Age dugout canoe

History is sometimes raised from the harbour waters. In August 1964 a dredger of the Poole Harbour Commissioners was at work in Brownsea Roads, off the island, and brought up a large block of sodden oak. This was twenty-three feet long and it turned out to be a dugout canoe with the stern virtually intact. A second part was located by divers in the harbour silt and recovered to complete the boat, measuring thirty-three feet from bow to stern, which was

COMPARATIVE MAPS

1980s

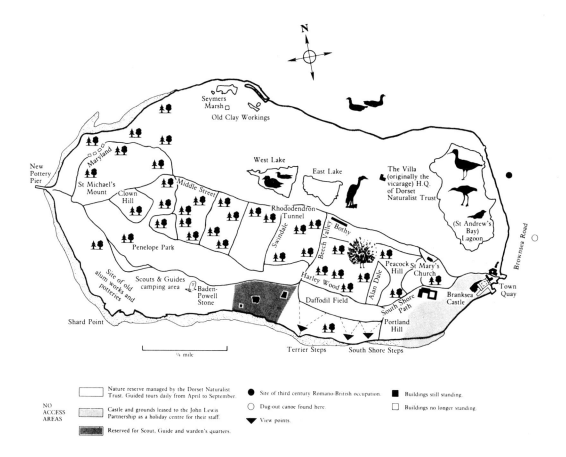

Map to the same scale (¼ mile = 23 mm) showing the wildlife emphasis of National Trust ownership. The white northern parts (shown as Cambridge Wood and Oxford Wood on the opposite page) are now a nature reserve with access restricted to daily guided tours. This zone includes the freshwater lakes and the saltwater lagoon of St. Andrew's Bay. Recent features include the Baden-Powell commemorative stone. Offshore blobs, in the anchorage of Brownsea Road on the east side of the island, show the discovery sites of the dug-out canoe that is described on this page and the Roman pottery mentioned overleaf.

Courtesy: National Trust

placed in a purpose-built tank of fresh water at Scaplen's Court, a museum in Poole. It was later gradually dried off before being finally treated with a polyethylene glycol preservative. The canoe is a monoxylon, a boat made from a single piece of timber, with two strengthened transverse ribs carved out of the floor. A groove in the stern shows that a 'stern-board' was used as a rudder. The boat was made about 300 BC in the Iron Age and is one of the most important maritime remains ever to be preserved.

Roman settlement at north-east corner

Brownsea Island's known past starts with the Romans. In 1973 Alan Bromby, the island's head warden, discovered Roman pottery and settlement debris at the extreme low point of spring tides some two hundred feet from the sea wall off the north-east corner of the island. It has been regarded as evidence of considerable tidal erosion, or alternatively a rise of six feet in the sea level since the late Roman period, and is most likely a combination of these factors.

Cnut and Brownsea, 1015

Thomas Gerard, writing in the 1620's though not published until almost a century later and then under a wrong name, John Coker, says that "Canutus, the Dane, after[wards] King of England, having spoiled the church and monasterie of Cerne, tooke to the haven and sailed thence to Branksey."

This is the Cnut [Canute] who will forever be associated with the tides, though no opportunity should be missed for trying to put the story right – he was demonstrating to his sillier acolytes that whatever they might suppose a king has no power over nature. He ravaged Dorset in 1015 – not 1014 as incorrectly given in many histories – and took over the kingdom in 1016. He died at Shaftesbury in 1035.

Brownsea's mediaeval hermitage of St Andrew

In mediaeval times, Brownsea was owned by the monks of Cerne Abbas who built a chapel and a hermitage there. It was dedicated to St. Andrew and the name survived at St. Andrew's Bay until that was drained and reclaimed by William Waugh in the early 1850s.

The religious buildings on Brownsea Island appear to have been in the area of the farm buildings, 150 yards west from the castle. There, on the castle side of the farm, seven skeletons have been dug up. They were beneath a sixteenth century layer, and one of the bones has been radio carbon dated to between 1100 and 1230. The cemetery would have been close to the monk's church, and used by the island families as well as the canons.

Henry VIII's castle, 1547

The strategic position of the island was exploited in 1547 when Henry VIII built a castle to protect Poole from seaborne attack by covering the narrow entrance to Poole Harbour. It was a square single-storey building with walls forty feet long and nine feet thick. On three sides the fort had a moat and the fourth, facing seaward, held a hexagonal gun platform. Brownsea was one of a string of coastal forts built by the king as part of the most extensive defence system along the English Channel since the Saxon shore forts of the Romans. To the west, at Portland Bay, Henry built Sandsfoot Castle and Portland Castle, and eastward, on a spit of shingle off Lymington, Hurst Castle was the strongest of them all to guard the important sealanes into the Solent. Brownsea alone was later to become a house but the greater part of the original fort is concealed in the basement of its eighteenth century tower.

HENRY VIII's CASTLE

Courtesy: B. A. Seaby Ltd

Cnut: Brownsea's first known visitor.

Photograph: Colin Graham

Right. Henry VIII's castle provides the foundations for the present Brownsea Castle. A future generation will have the initiative to strip the plaster and reveal the stonework. For now it is the laundry and boiler house.

Below. Henry VIII's defence map of Poole Harbour showing a ship sailing by the eastern end of Brownsea Island having just passed through the harbour entrance. At the bottom there is a plan of the 'gun castle' and a drawing of its platform. One was built at the east end of Brownsea, in a direct line with the harbour mouth, and another (since lost into the sea by coast erosion) on the north-east corner of Handfast Point (known to us as Old Harry Rocks) to the east of Studland. The dark line projecting north-eastwards from there, across the sea, indicates the field of fire. England prepared for invasion after Henry had split from the Church of Rome.

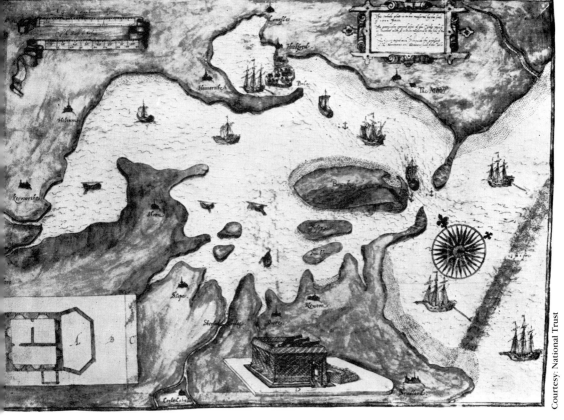
Courtesy: National Trust

Elizabeth I in a gold medal of 1572. 'The Defence of the Kingdom' is the theme. The reverse shows a castle on a mount. Her castle at Brownsea she gave to Sir Christopher Hatton, who was far from being a favourite with the harbour ferrymen.

Brownsea's real history followed the building of the castle. Queen Elizabeth I made a life gift of it to Sir Christopher Hatton who was described as "a mere vegetable of the Court, that sprang up in the night". He was constantly in dispute with the townspeople of Poole and took revenge on them by confiscating the fishermen's traditional ferrying rights between the Sandbanks and South Haven Peninsula of Purbeck. An admiralty court decided against him in 1581 but the fact that the dispute went to law indicates that this communications link between Poole and eastern Purbeck was important from an early time.

'Bad fellow of odious religion' in Brownsea mines 1586

The extent of the deteriorating relationship between Poole and Brownsea is shown by the following whine from the mayor and corporation of Poole to Sir Francis Ashley, concerning the religious disinclinations of the Brownsea miners. It is dated 4 February 1586:

> These are to advertise you, that we do know James Mounsey, of London, who farmeth the mines of Brownsea, at my lord of Huntingdon's hands, and this man whom you have sent is the same Mounsey, whose religion we doubt, for that we have not seen him at any time at the church in the time of his being here. He hath a brother, a very bad fellow, and of an odious religion, who serveth in Brownsea mines under him. He persuadeth the workmen there to labour the Sabbath day, and to rest the Saturday, which he saith is the Sabbath day. We understand this Mounsey to be indebted to the victuallers of this town and the workmen of the Brownsea mines. It may please your worship to have regard to Brownsea Castle; it is a place of great danger, and weakly manned, which may give ingress and egress to the enemy, to the prejudice of the whole country, not being foreseen to be provided with credible persons for the defence of that charge.

Philip Brannon's detailed description of Brownsea in his informative 'Guide to Poole and Bournemouth' of 1857 suggests that this former industrial activity was carried on along the central southern shore, in the area of South Shore Lodge and Barnes' Bottom: "Below, on a piece of level land between the bank and the water were some kilns, which are now destroyed. Not far from this were discovered, in carrying on the works, some of the old cisterns formed on solid oak staves, which had been used in the former alum and copperas works we have mentioned in the historical remarks. It is most probable, too, that on this low land were some of the salterns supposed to have been in the island. On the rolling land between the ridge and the water are placed some detached cottages for the forester and gamekeepers of the estate, and it is intended near them to erect a laundry, fowl-house, and kennel."

The shelling of 'Bountiful Gift', 1589

When Tudor England was in a state of post Armada nerves, Francis Hawley, the vice-admiral of Dorset who was stationed at Corfe Castle, was ordered with other officers responsible for the coast that no vessels should pass out of his harbours except boats making for other English ports. He was given power to strip suspected vessels of their sails. A result of this order was a shooting incident that occurred in February 1589 when Walter Partridge, commander of Brownsea Castle, rejected a pass presented by the master of the *Bountiful Gift*, a barque leaving Poole Harbour with a cargo of copperas. The vessel refused to stay and the castle battery fired two shots. The master, Walter Merritt, and one of his men, William Drake, were killed and a coroner's inquest at Corfe returned a verdict of wilful murder against Partridge. He later had to stand trial at a special court, was found guilty of manslaughter and sentenced to death "without the benefit of clergy" as the felony was committed at sea. But Partridge, not unfairly, was granted a pardon in December 1590 on the ground that the shots were intended only "to stay the sail ship".

The town of Poole joined the Parliamentary side in the Civil War and Brownsea Castle was strongly armed and garrisoned at an early stage. Four large guns and several chests of muskets were delivered for a force that in February 1645 was twenty strong. When the first phase of the Civil War was at an end, money due to the victor's armies for special services was settled. Poole had successfully held out against the royalists throughout the struggle and £60 was granted to the Brownsea garrison in April 1647.

Brunksey and the islands of 'Nymphidia', 1613

The three major islands of Poole Harbour are anthropomorphised in 'Poly-olbion', the celebrated topographical description of the English counties, in twelve-syllabled verse, published in 1613 by Michael Drayton [1563-1631].

The islands of "Brunksey; Fursey next; and little [Saint] Hellen [now Green Island] last" are the children of "Great Albyon"; begat of Poole when she was "a lustie Sea-borne lass, Great Albyon to this Nymph an earnest suter was ..."

This epic fairyland poem, 'Nymphidia', is accompanied by a map of Dorset and Hampshire. It is among the rarest of local antique maps – the book went through only one edition – and certainly the most unusual. It features the page three girls of its day, standing on the three islands in Poole Harbour and arising from the district's rivers and forests. Appendices to the poems explain the rationale; particularly the associations with classical mythology. These antiquarian asides were added by John Selden.

A further batch of songs, though without the benefit of Selden's fascinating annotations, were published in 1622. Drayton had been helped by William Drummond, to whom he wrote in 1619: "I thank you, my dear, sweet Drummond, for your good opinion of 'Poly-olbion'. I have done twelve books more; ... but it lieth by me, for the booksellers and I are in terms [dispute]. They are a company of base knaves, whom I both scorn and kick at. Dear, sweet Michael Drayton, I understand so well."

Merely quoting from 'Poly-olbion' conveys next to nothing of its scope and beauty so in the next three pages I will reproduce the full page with the Brownsea mentions together with the relevant map and Selden's notes.

POLY-OLBION,

WHen *Poole* (quoth shee) was young, a lustie Sea-borne Lasse,
Great *Albyon* to this Nymph an earnest suter was;
And bare himselfe so well, and so in fauour came,
That he in little time, vpon this louelie Dame
§. Begot three mayden Iles, his darlings and delight :
The eldest, *Brunksey* call'd; the second, *Fursey* hight;
The youngest and the last, and lesser then the other,
Saint *Hellens* name doth beare, the dilling of her Mother.
And, for the goodlie *Poole* was one of *Thetis* traine,
Who scorn'd a Nymph of hers, her Virgin-band should staine,
Great *Albyon* (that fore-thought, the angrie Goddesse would
Both on the Dam and brats take what reuenge shee could)
I'th bosome of the *Poole* his little children plac't :
First, *Brunksey*; *Fursey* next; and little *Hellen* last;
Then, with his mightie armes doth clip the *Poole* about,
To keepe the angrie Queene, fierce *Amphitrite* out.
Against whose lordlie might shee musters vp her waues;
And strongly thence repulst (with madnes) scoulds and raues.
  When now, from *Poole*, the Muse (vp to her pitch to get)
Her selfe in such a place from sight doth almost set,
As by the actiue power of her commanding wings,
She (Falcon-like) from farre doth fetch those plentious Springs.
Where *Stour* receiues her strength frō * sixe cleere Fountaines fed;
Which gathering to one streame from euery seuerall head,
Her new-beginning banke her water scarcely weelds;
And fairelie entreth first on the *Dorsetian* feelds :
Where *Gillingham* with gifts that for a God were meet
(Enameld paths, rich wreaths, and euery soueraine sweet
The earth and ayre can yeeld, with many a pleasure mixt)
Receiues her. Whilst there past great kindnes them betwixt,
The Forrest her bespoke; How happie floods are yee,
From our predestin'd plagues that priuiledged bee;
Which onelie with the fish which in your banks doe breed,
And dailie there increase, mans gurmandize can feed?
But had this wretched Age such vses to imploy
Your waters, as the woods we latelie did enioy,
Your chanels they would leaue as barren by their spoile,
As they of all our trees haue lastlie left our soile.
Insatiable Time thus all things doth deuour :
What euer saw the sunne, that is not in Times power?
Yee fleeting Streames last long, out-liuing manie a day :
But, on more stedfast things Time makes the strongest pray.
  §. Now tow'rds the *Solent* sea as *Stour* her way doth ply,
On *Shaftsbury* (by chance) shee cast her crystall eye,
From whose foundation first, such strange reports arise
§. As brought into her mind the *Eagles* prophecies

The storie of Poole.

* Stour riseth from six fountaines.

Opposite and above. **'The storie of Poole' from the 'Nymphidia' of Michael Drayton's 'Poly-olbion', 1613. The map shows the local nymphs, including 'Brunksey, Fursey, St Hellen' representing the main islands of Poole Harbour.**
Source: Rodney Legg collection

On whom the watry God *would oft haue had his will.*

Purbeck (named, but indeed not, an Iſle, being ioynd to the firme land) ſtored with game of the Forreſt.

Thence alluding to *Diana's* deuotions, the author well cals her an *Huntres* and a *Nunne*. Nor doth the embracing force of the Ocean (whereto ſhe is adiacent) although very violent, preuaile againſt her ſtonie cliffes. To this purpoſe the Muſe is heere wanton with *Neptunes* wooing.

That he in little time vpon this lonely dame,
Begat three maiden Iſles *his darlings and delight.*

Albion (ſonne of *Neptune*) from whom that firſt name of this *Britaine* was ſuppoſed, is well fitted to the fruitfull bedde of this *Poole*, thus perſonated as a Sea Nymph. The plaine truth (as wordes may certifie your eyes, ſauing all impropriety of obiect) is, that in the *Poole* are ſeated three Iſles, *Brunkſey, Furſey,* and *S. Helens*, in ſituation and magnitude, as I name them. Nor is the fiction of begetting the Iſles improper; ſeeing Greek [h] antiquities tell vs of diuers in the *Mediterranean* and the *Archipelag*, as *Rhodes, Delos, Hiera,* the *Echinades*, and others, which haue beene, as it were, brought forth out of the ſalt womb of *Amphitrite.*

But towards the Solent *Sea, as* Stour *her way doth ply,*
On Shaftsbury, *&c.*

The ſtraight twixt the *Wight* and *Hantſhire*, is titled in *Bedes* ſtory, *Pelagus latitudinis* III. *millium quod vocatur Solente;* famous for the double, and therby moſt violent flouds of the Ocean (as *Scylla* & *Charybdis* twixt *Sicily* and *Italy* in *Homer*) expreſſed by the Author towards the end of this Song, & reckon'd among our *Britiſh* wonders. Of it the Author tels you more preſently. Concerning *Shaftesbury* (which, beſide other names, [i] from the corps of S[t]*. Edward,* murdred in *Corfe* Caſtle, through procurement of the bloudy hate of his ſtepmother *Ælfrith*, hither tranſlated, and ſome III. yeares lying buried, was once called S[t]*. Edwards*) you ſhall heare a peece out of *Harding* ; .

[k] Caire Paladoure that now is Shafteſbury
Where an Angell ſpake ſitting on the wall
While it was in workying ouer all.

Iſles newly out of the Sea.
[h] *Lucian dialog. Pindar.olymp.*3*. Strab.Pauſanias.*

* A Sea three miles ouer, called *Solente.lib.*4 *hiſt. eccleſ.cap.* 16.

[i] *Malmesb.lib.* 2.*de Pontific.* *S.Edwards.* DCCCC.LXXIX.

[k] *Camden* takes this Cair for *Bath.*

The rationale for Michael Drayton's fairyland, added by John Selden as an appendix to the Dorset section of the epic poem, 'Nymphidia', from the 'Poly-olbion'.

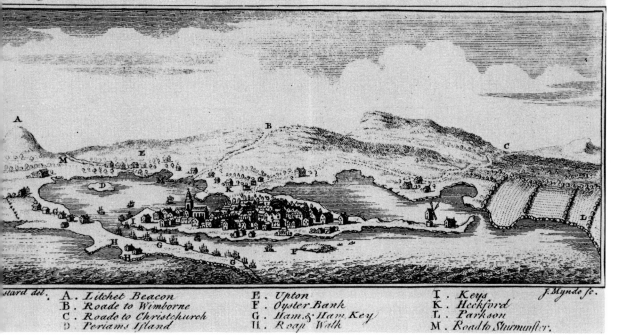

Back to reality after all the nudes fit to print ... a very boring print of Poole, a prospect from the Maryland end of Brownsea Island, which shows that the island had a strategic value for the defence of the port. It is from John Hutchins's County History.

Source: Rodney Legg collection

Thomas Pride on Brownsea, 1654

There is a record of Colonel Thomas Pride and some of his regiment of the Commonwealth army being stationed on Brownsea in 1654. Most of his troops had been sent to Scotland. Pride's place in history is at the turning point of seventeenth century politics. Charles I, after his forces were finally defeated at Preston in the second part of the English Civil War, spent weeks at Newport, Isle of Wight, pleading for a treaty. He lied, he evaded, and he procrastinated. That he never intended honouring his concessions is clear from his own admission. His offers were "made merely in order to effect my escape, of which, if I had not hope, I would not have done ... for my hope is that they now believe I dare deny them nothing, and so be less careful of their guards."

The army saw the achievements of its victory being talked away in a spate of politicians' words. On 30 November 1648 the original colonels' revolt was initiated. Charles had his escape plan thwarted and was removed across the Solent to Hurst Castle on 1 December. The next day the army marched into London. The excuse needed for stage three of the revolt was provided when the Presbyterian members of the House of Commons voted that the king's preposterous suggestions amounted to grounds "for the settlement of the peace of the kingdom". The following day was "Pride's purge". Colonel Pride, on orders from Sir Thomas Fairfax, stationed his men at the door to the Commons and prevented eighty Presbyterians taking their seats. The

Independent Rump of the Commons then rejected any idea of reinstating the king and instead set up a revolutionary tribunal. Charles was beheaded at Whitehall on 30 January 1649 and the monarchy and the House of Lords were abolished.

Charles I: a 1649 memorial medal by John Roettier. The crown was now up in the clouds.
Courtesy: B. A. Seaby Ltd

Brownsea was then garrisoned throughout the Commonwealth when there was a need for the defence of Poole Harbour. In 1655 a light boat without decks, described as a "shallop man-of-man", approached some of the boats of George Skutt, Governor of Brownsea Castle. Though caught by surprise they managed to take the intruding vessel and found it had a commission from James, the second son of Charles I, who later became James II of England. The restoration of the monarchy in 1660 led to the end of Brownsea as a castle in the military sense.

Charles II: he was rowed around Brownsea in 1665, though to kill time rather than enjoy it. London was then the Plague City. The medal aspires to designs on more distant islands – 'DIFFVSVS IN ORBE BRITANNVS' ... a celebration of British colonisation. It too is by John Roettier.
Courtesy: B. A. Seaby Ltd

Charles II and Monmouth rowed round Brownsea

The island's next contact with national affairs came on 15 September 1665 when Charles II and his son James, Duke of Monmouth, were rowed round the island. They were resting in Poole after a hasty journey from London to escape the plague. But the visitors did not land on isolated Brownsea Island, the reason being probably that the island's owner was Sir Robert Clayton, one of the wealthiest men in the City of London, who had loaned Charles vast sums. Clayton rarely came to the island but may also have fled from London that summer. At any rate the king had forgotten to repay £30,000 that was borrowed to pay his soldiers. There appears to have been a large house on the island at this time, though by 1800 it was in ruins, and now only two brick walls and the piers that supported a gateway are preserved in the courtyard of an old dairy building west of the castle.

Revival of copperas manufactory, 1690s

Sir Robert Clayton, as would be expected, attempted to make money out of the island and reopened the sixteenth century copperas works. Copperas is a sulphate of iron, known also as green vitriol, that was used in dyeing, tanning, painting and making ink. As Brownsea's entire industrial history is one of misfortunes, this venture is unlikely to have been successful.

Celia Fiennes, one of the great female explorers, took in Brownsea on her "Great Journey" through Britain in 1698-99. She provides a remarkably detailed account of the island off Poole, with unique details of the copperas manufactory:

> From thence by boate we went to a little Isle called Brownsea 3 or 4 leagues off, where there is much Copperice [copperas] made, the stone being found about the Isle in the shore in great quantetyes, there is only one house which is the Governours, besides little fishermen houses, they being all taken up about the Copperice workers; they gather the stones and place them on ground raised like the beds in gardens, rows one above the other, and are all shelving so that the raine disolves the stones and it draines down into trench and pipes made to receive and convey it to the house; that is fitted with iron panns foursquare and of a pretty depth at least 12 yards over, they place iron spikes in the panns full of branches and so as the liquor boyles to a candy it hangs on those branches: I saw some taken up it look't like a vast bunch of grapes, the coullour of the Copperace not being much differing, it looks cleare like sugar-candy, so when the water is boyled to a candy they take it out and replenish the panns with more liquor; I do not remember they added anything to it only the stones of Copperice disolved by the raine into liquour as I mention'd at first; there are great furnaces under, that keepes all the panns boyling; it was a large room or building with severall of these large panns; they do add old iron and nailes to the Copperass Stones. This is a noted place for lobsters and crabs and shrimps, there I eate some very good.

Mad Benson's reign, 1710-54

Sometime after his death in 1707, probably about 1710, Sir Robert Clayton's heirs sold the island to William Benson. He paid £300 and considered he had also bought the castle which, actually, was still crown property. Furthermore, he knew it was. Complaints were made by the people of Poole who asked George II to reclaim the castle: but Benson moved in high places and he outwitted the objectors. Possession being almost everything, and especially so with a castle, he treated the place as his own and promptly started work to add a "great hall" to the fort. In 1711, Benson created a national stir by publishing his 'Letter to Sir Jacob Bankes'. This argued that kings were accountable only to God, and sold 100,000 copies.

Benson's hobbies were a little ahead of his time and he utilised the island for the growth of rare botanical specimens and planted various species of trees. He also sponsored the arts and printed Samuel Johnson's 'Psalms' as well as erecting a monument to the memory of John Milton (deceased, 1674) in Westminster Abbey. For these two acts he was lampooned by Alexander Pope: "On two unequal crutches propp'd he came, Milton's on this, on that one Johnson's name." Pope rams the point home: "On poets' tombs see Benson's titles writ".

By the end of 1741, Benson had suffered a nervous breakdown and had to be restrained. He recovered but his "former love of books had given way to a positive hatred" and he was known as "Mad Benson" until his death in 1754. Benson's friends had included Frederick, Prince of Wales, who visited Brownsea a few months before the owner's breakdown. Frederick, a popular prince, never took the throne as he failed to outlive his unpopular father. Bernard Short wrote in his booklet 'Brownsea Island' that many believed Benson practised black magic and that the island was used for necromancy and the meetings of witches' covens:

> It is said that the celebration of the black mass took place in some pine-clad grove. In 1735, a servant girl vanished from the island, and it was strongly rumoured in Poole that she had been sacrificed to some satanic power at one of Benson's hideous ceremonies. Fishermen came back to the town saying that they had heard blood curdling screams ringing forth from Brownsea, and moreover, there had been glimmerings of lights in the woods. Certainly the servant girl from the island was never heard of again. But perhaps she merely absconded from the island without anyone knowing, and as for the screams they might well have been the shriek of a bird such as a screech owl.

Humphrey Sturt rebuilt the castle

The island entered a phase of improvements when it came into the hands of the Sturt family of More Crichel. Humphrey Sturt, who sat for Dorset in the Commons, took on Brownsea in 1765 and set about turning it into the country estate extraordinary. He built up the castle into a four-storey tower with wings branching off on four sides. The grounds he transformed into ornamental gardens and all across the island he planted trees. By this time there was some semblance of a community as the island had a coastguard station and a public house. Sturt poured some £50,000 into his various schemes and the family kept the island for thirty years after his death. It was sold to Sir Charles Chad who held the island until 1840 and built the cottages called Seymer's House, now in ruins, overlooking the northern shore.

To farming commentator Arthur Young, who never missed an opportunity to make exaggerated claims for the agricultural potential of the infertile southern heaths, Brownsea offered an offshore utopia. He enthused about the island in 'The Farmer's Tour through England', published 1770:

> Brownsea, near Poole consists of nine hundred acres of land, quite wild and over-run with fern, furze and much ling. It was esteemed so very poor and little worth

Opposite. **Brownsea Castle, as rebuilt by Humphrey Sturt, drawn by J. P. Neale in 1822. The sea view is from the north-east, across the anchorage of Brownsea Road, but the ancilliary buildings appear in mirror image – they should stretch out to the right, not the left. The other view is correct, from the south, and shows the north side of the Castle with a line of cannon pointing towards the harbour entrance.**

Following pages. **Print of Brownsea Castle, dated 1793, from the west (the island side, showing St. Andrew's Bay which was later drained). It is from the Second Edition of John Hutchins's County History of which only 112 sets were produced. It has been since rendered unobtainable by interior decorators who masquerade as booksellers, and their customers who fail to realise that each print they purchase from these vandals sends another book to the butcher's knife.**

Source: Rodney Legg collection, from one of the very few intact copies

Drawn by J.P.Neale. Engraved by T.Matthews.
BROWNSEA CASTLE.
(GENERAL VIEW)
DORSETSHIRE.

Source: Rodney Legg collection

Drawn by J.P.Neale. Engraved by H.Hobson.
BROWNSEA CASTLE.
DORSETSHIRE.

BROWNSEA: DORSET'S FANTASY ISLAND

South East View of Brownsea Castle & Island.

Print from the Victorian Third Edition of John Hutchins's County History of Dorsetshire. This is still Sturt's Castle, flying an outsized Union Jack. It is seen from Sandbanks, as the North Haven Peninsula is now known. Poole town is glimpsed to the top right.
Source: Rodney Legg collection

that it was, with difficulty, let to a butcher at Poole for £16 a year; and the only use he made of it was to turn on a few lean sheep now and then.

In this state Mr Sturt purchased it, and immediately set about its improvement with great spirit and equal judgement. Besides building the Castle he has planted the sides of the hills with various sorts of firs to the number of a million. These thrive well. The vales and flat lands are improved by degrees, fifty acres laid to white clover and hay seed, that shew how well the land will do for pasture and meadow. The soil is, in general, a black, moory, peat earth, on various strata, either sand, gravel or loam; but the new-laid fields do equally well on all, which shews that the black soil itself is sufficiently good for the purpose. The grass annually improves. I never have seen finer clover – thicker, more luxuriant, or that promised better to be most profitable land. The whole Mr Sturt has laid is extremely well worth paying twenty shillings an acre.

... there is no production which tends to render a country profitable, agreeable or convenient, but what may be found in great plenty on this happy island, which is really England in miniature.

Sir Augustus Foster slits his throat in Branksea Castle, 1848

Augustus John Foster was born on 1 December 1780. Through the influence of his mother, re-married and now the Duchess of Devonshire, he would find his career as a civil servant beginning with his appointment as secretary to the British legation in Naples. From there he received a sensitive and major appointment that was beyond his abilities and in which he would prove to be a disaster. He was dispatched in August 1811 to Washington as Minister Plenipotentiary on behalf of the Court of St James to the United States of America.

In temperament he was not a diplomat at all and he failed to sort out the simmering row over the impressment of American seamen into the Royal Navy for the war against France. America had seized its independence in the war of 1775-80 and felt that its neutrality was being compromised. Foster was arrogant and beligerent in his defence of the British orders in council, signed in 1807, that had brought about the dispute. Matters came to a head in June 1812.

Foster failed to hold the situation at a time when in reality there was no longer any dispute. London had backed down on the 16th and withdrawn the contentious orders. Washington was unaware of any such conciliatory mood, as none was apparent in our minister, and declared war against the British on the 18th. They prepared to invade Canada. That offensive was outmanoeuvred and British troops in North America came south to burn the Capitol in 1813 and destroy most of the Library of Congress.

The great American victory of the war did not come about until 1815, and then two weeks after the Treaty of Ghent had ended the hostilities. Jean Laffite, the French pirate, had tipped off the defenders of New Orleans about imminent sea-borne landings which were then decisively countered with 700 British dead and 1,400 wounded for the loss of eight American dead and thirteen wounded. As for Foster, having won his place in history as the last man to put us at war with the United States of America, his continuation of diplomacy by other means met with the standard protocol; he was sent packing. Back in England he entered Parliament, as MP for Cockermouth, and in May 1814 was at sea again, to Copenhagen as Minister Plenipotentiary to Denmark. This was a posting of no consequence – which was why he was given it – and Foster settled down to married life with Albinia Jane Hobart and in 1822 was allowed on to the Privy Council. In 1824 he was posted to Turin and received a knighthood the following year.

Sir Augustus again avoided starting another war and London left him in Italy for sixteen years. His conduct was rewarded with a baronetcy and on retirement in 1840 he bought Brownsea Island from Sir Charles Chad.

Far from finding paradise he fell into bouts of deep depression. These steadily became more intense as his general health deteriorated. The last was on 1 August 1848 when he was at home in Branksea Castle – the contemporary form of the island's name – and he ended it by slitting his throat.

The Gentleman's Magazine records:

> Sir Augustus Foster, Bt; At an inquest held on the body of the deceased, it appeared that he had for several months been suffering from disease of the heart and lungs,

BROWNSEA: DORSET'S FANTASY ISLAND

The Castle and Quay complex of Brownsea Island in 1876, from across the pastures of a (temporarily) drained St Andrew's Bay.
Courtesy: Dorset County Magazine

St Mary's church, in 1876, from across the lawn on its south side. The vegetation was not yet out of control.

and had recently laboured under delirium, during a fit of which he destroyed himself by cutting his throat. A verdict was returned of temporary insanity.

His widow stayed on the island and the next era awaited a visit from Colonel and Mrs William Petrie Waugh, late of the XXth [East Devonshire] Regiment of Foot and the Indian Army, in 1853.

Draining of St Andrew's Bay, 1853

Brownsea's heyday came when Colonel William Waugh bought the island in 1852, from the executors of Sir Augustus Foster, for £13,000. This price was far higher than the earlier sales figures but Waugh had a special reason for wanting the property. His wife had made a hobby of geology and she picked and prodded at the ground with her umbrella to reveal potters' clay. Her opinion of its potential value was endorsed by a professional geologist who reported "a most valuable bed of the finest clay" worth "at a low computation, at least £100,000 an acre".

Waugh was certain that the porcelain of the future would be made with Brownsea clay - "the richest" in the United Kingdom. He was able to back his hunch with the money of others. As a director of the London and Eastern Banking Corporation he had no dificulty in raising £237,000 with the island as security. As an economist, Waugh had doubtful priorities. He not only restored and embellished the castle but wasted a further £10,000 in 1853 on erecting the church which is still standing on the edge of the island woods. An even more wasteful project was the reclamation of St Andrew's Bay which needed countless barge-loads of subsoil and more than a million bricks to add a hundred acres to the island. Its meadows remained watery, and have now fully reverted to marshland.

Sir William Waugh's 1853-54 transformation of Brownsea, with a promenade along the sea wall (right) across the former St. Andrew's Bay. There is also a new gothic Castle, more castellated quayside cottages, and a church at the edge of the woods. The drawing is by Philip Brannon, about 1860.
Source: Rodney Legg collection

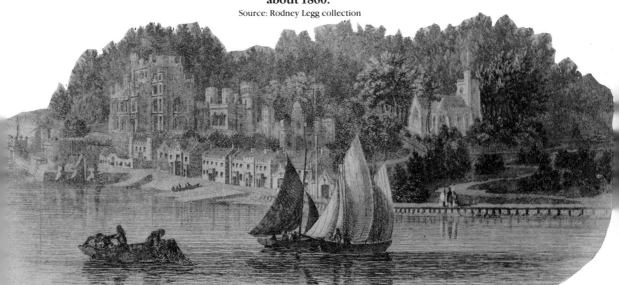

The great Victorian occasions, 1853-54

A thousand guests were ferried across to witness the laying of the foundation stone to St Mary's church, which was close to the site of the "chappel for an heremite" that John Hutchins recorded in 1774. The Poole and South-Western Herald noted that Colonel William Petrie Waugh had "taken particular care to preserve the small portion of the chapel wall which still remains" – though no one has since been able to re-discover it.

The great occasions of 1853 and 1854, when the church was completed and consecrated, were recorded by Reverend Theophilus Bennett in 1881. He does not mention that Sir Percy Florence Shelley, the poet's only surviving son [1819-89], was in attendance in 1854 with Lady Shelley. They lived at Boscombe Manor, Bournemouth. The account shows that inevitably a hymn was selected for its mention of "our Island home", and another specially composed for the consecration:

> On Saturday, 2nd of July, 1853, the foundation stone of St. Mary's, Brownsea Island, was laid by Major-General Sir Harry Smith, G.C.B.
>
> A Hymn composed by a lady for the occasion, was sung immediately after the repetition of the Lord's Prayer.
>
> The following was the hymn:-
>
>> May all assembled here to-day
>>   Their cheerful voices raise,
>> And with thanksgiving to the Lord
>>   Now sing a Hymn of praise.
>>
>> The first foundation stone is laid,
>>   An Edifice to rear,
>> Where we may humbly worship God
>>   On every Sabbath here.
>>
>> Let us devoutly pray to Him
>>   Who reigns in heaven above,
>> To send a blessing on his work
>>   Begun in faith and love.
>>
>> Glad Hallelujahs let us raise
>>   Unto God's praise on High:
>> And oh! May his Almighty arm
>>   With us be ever nigh.
>>
>> May Christ, the Great Redeemer, prove
>>   The Stepherd of His flock;
>> To guard us in our Island home
>>   Our everlasting rock.
>
> The Church itself stands on a beautifully selected site in the midst of a clump of lofty fir trees on the north-eastern part of the Island. It is surrounded by "God's Acre," adorned with neat monuments and bright cheerful little gardens, for if there was a sepulchre in the garden, why should there not be a garden in the sepulchre? And on Wednesday, the 18th Oct., 1854 there was a holy solemnity when this church and church-yard were set apart for ever from all secular uses to the service of Almighty God. The Right Reverend Bishop Hamilton consecrated, and then the following hymn, composed expressly for the occasion by Miss Maxwell, with music by E. Brown, Esq., was sung –

Island battlements: the Quay.
Photograph: Colin Graham

> Within the courts of God's own house
>   We meet on this auspicious day,
> To celebrate the finished work
>   Where we may praise God's name and pray.
> The solemn consecration o'er,
>   With true devotion let us sing
> Hosannah to the Lord on High,
>   Glory to Christ our Heavenly King.
> Now with thank-offerings of joy
>   Let great Jehovah's name be praised,
> For, dedicated her to Him,
>   A temple to the Lord is raised.
> May holy love within our hearts
>   Burn with a bright and heavenly flame,
> And ever in our island Church
>   Adored be our Redeemer's name.

On the handsome urns that stand on the Churchyard gate are inscribed in old English characters the words:-
1. Ask, and ye shall receive.
2. Seek and ye shall find. Knock and it shall be opened.

Brownsea's echo of the Princes in the Tower

The most remarkable of the treasures that have found their way to Brownsea Island is the splendid 1446 ceiling of twelve panels removed from Crosby Place, Bishopsgate. This was brought to the island in 1853-54 to roof Colonel William Waugh's private chapel, which is an adjunct to the north-east side of St Mary's church.

Crosby Place was built by grocer and wool merchant John Crosby and was in its time the highest hall in London. The panels are from the main ceiling of the hall. Richard III [1452-85, King from 1483] lived there when he was Duke of Gloucester. The hall in Bishopsgate Street became the meeting place for the conspirators of the age, who commissioned some of the most heinous excesses of English history, as Richard abused his position as Protector – standing in for his thirteen-year-old son Edward V who was, with his brother, to be murdered in the Tower of London.

The chapel ceiling is therefore Brownsea's link with real history. It has heard treason and the announcement of the death of the princes.

By mid-Victorian times, Crosby Place had fallen from its heady days of State schisms. It was being converted into a restaurant and the final demolitions followed in 1908.

Opposite. [Top left]. **The Clocktower.** [Top right]. **The nave of St Mary's church, which was consecrated on 18 October 1854.** [Below]. **Stained glass in the chancel window.**
Photographs: Colin Graham

Below. **The newly-built St Mary's church, drawn from the north-east by Philip Brannon about 1860. The nearside projection is Colonel Waugh's private chapel.**
Source: Rodney Legg collection

CLOCKTOWER AND CHURCH

Left. **The seventeenth century painting of the Crucifixion in the private chapel is Italian and the candelabrum dates from the eighteenth century. It is the roof, however, that is the real treasure. The panels are from the 1446 ceiling of Crosby Place, Bishopsgate.**

Below. **St Mary's church still stands in the trees. This view is from the south-east and the projection from the base of the tower is the memorial chapel added by Mrs Florence van Raalte in 1908.**
Photographs: Colin Graham

Opposite. **The gothic turrets of William Petrie Waugh's 1853 rebuilding of Brownsea Castle, in a contemporary print which shows bussle at the quayside.**
Source: Rodney Legg collection

Opposite, bottom. **The view across St. Andrew's Bay, reclaimed by the sea as soon as the pumping ceased, which Colonel Waugh had drained. His sea wall of a million bricks is now a causeway. On the mud there are rafts of cormorant and oystercatcher. Across the harbour, the Poole skyline is dominated by a mid 1970s fortress of mammon – the towers of Barclays House (headquarters of Barclays Bank International Ltd).**
Photograph: Colin Graham

Quay Cottages, seen from the Quay with the Poole shoreline in the distance.

Photographs: Colin Graham

The quayside waiting room, with Quay Cottages glimpsed to the right.

The main Quay at the east end of Brownsea, with Quay Cottages to the right, seen from the north.

Photographs: Colin Graham

Brownsea Pottery and Maryland Village, 1855

The western side of the island was devoted to an industrial complex that had to earn sufficient to keep up the ten percent interest repayments on the loans. Brownsea Pottery was built at the south-west corner of the island, opposite Furzey Island, and produced pottery, bricks and tiles. There was a two-storey processing unit with workshops, ranges of kilns, and several subsidiary buildings. The tall brick chimney above the main set of kilns was one of the harbour's landmarks. A short distance away, below Red Hill, was a smaller pottery and stables. A pier was built there but soon replaced by Pottery Pier a little further north. Maryland Village, a crescent of cottages for clayworkers, was built by Colonel Waugh in 1855 and named after his wife.

Further away, on the middle of the northern shore, was the main clayfield where numerous shafts were sunk. A brickworks lay to the east of Seymer's Pier. The whole enterprise was linked by a tramway that ran westward from the brickworks to Maryland, Pottery Pier, the smaller pottery, and then branched into sidings at Brownsea Pottery. The railway kept to the level land beside the shore and was over a mile long.

Seymour's [now spelt 'Seymer's'] Point was described by Philip Brannon in his 1857 'Guide to Poole and Bournemouth':

> It is marked by a cottage pleasantly creating the high bank, amongst scattered groups of firs. It has been for a short time used as a parsonage house, but a residence for the clergyman being erected nearer to the church, it is now the residence of Mr Petts, the intelligent and excellent manager of the works. At the foot of the ascent a great quantity of clay has been excavated; at this place it is got out from perpendicular shafts, about seventy-five feet deep, and twelve to fifteen feet square. The clay to this depth is a solid mass, varying perhaps a little irregularly, but in the following order from the top: – strong brown clay for stone ware; white ditto; white clay becoming yellow on the surface after exposure to the atmosphere, but which would make good white ware; fine strong clay stained with mottled colours; a fine blue or porcelain clay, etc.

The pottery, on the south-west point of the island facing the eastern third of Furzey Island, is also included in Brannon's account:

> The *Coarse Pottery*; it stands near the water's edge, and is sheltered by the high land to the north. It has been in very good taste broken in its form as much as such an establishment could well be, and is thus an ornamental addition to the scene. The building is intended solely for the production of strong coarse stone-ware, and is at present, like the other potteries in the district, almost wholly occupied in the production of glazed draining pipes. The two steam engines, the working stones for the crushing of the old material and dried clay, the powerful pug mills, and indeed the whole of the machinery, are of the most improved and excellent construction. There are several well-built kilns, and all the usual facilities for the perfect preparation of the material, and its being lifted to the upper floors, etc. On the first floor the moulding is executed, and here from sixty to two hundred and forty lengths of pipe, according to diameter, can be produced in an hour. Attached to the main building are drying sheds, six hundred feet long by twenty-five feet, and tramways communicate with all parts of the buildings, and skirting the south-west and north sides of the island connect all the different works and clay-pits.

Branksea Pottery – the 'Large Pottery and Brick Tile Works' with its manufactory and kilns at the south-west corner of the island. The water colour [above] is probably by Philip Brannon and dates from about 1858-59. The photograph is later, probably about 1880. Both views are from the western end of the southern perimeter path, between Penelope Park and St. Michael's Mount. Nothing now remains.

Following the line of the rail we presently arrive at ...
The *Terra Cotta and Architectural Pottery*. – These works are now completed, and it is proposed besides the nine kilns now erected, to put up an additional square or Scotch kiln. There is every material required for the production of the various articles now manufactured or proposed to be made here. Every variety of clay, from the coarsest brick earth to the finest blue porcelain, ochre for colouring, and sharpest sand to assist in the formation of fire-bricks, are dug close at hand, whilst several piers carry the tramway out to the verge of the deep-water channels. These potteries will therefore possess greater advantages than most other works, in respect to the proximity both of the material and points of shipment, in the manufacture of all the ordinary articles of stoneware. Fire-bricks and lumps equal to those of Stourbridge, and terra cotta and architectural works of all descriptions, are already being manufactured here. Whether they will ultimately embrace the finer descriptions of pottery it would be impossible now to say, but we cannot avoid expressing the belief, that the time is not very far distant when these manufactures will be introduced successfully in this district, and Branksea would in all probability be a point at which they would early [first] be established.

Thousands of tons of stoneware pipes lie in banks of up to eight feet high, on the shore opposite the west end of Furzey Island. The entire beach is strewn for more than four hundred yards with broken pottery and vitrified bricks from the linings of the kilns. Foundations of the pottery can be traced in grassland, directly opposite the boathouse at the centre of Furzey Island.

Waugh's bank crashes — flees to Spain, 1857

A surprise came in 1856 whilst Waugh was away in London at meetings of his bank. A number of Poole tradesmen landed on the island and were received by the colonel's wife. They had come to invite her husband to stand for Parliament and offered the seat of Poole. Being deaf, she was at a disadvantage, and thought they had come to demand payment of overdue accounts. The visitors were staggered when she begged for time to pay.

That was the first the people of Poole knew about the impending crash. The difficulties had arisen because the London and Eastern Banking Corporation was on the brink of insolvency. Shareholders turned on William Waugh for voting himself huge loans and ordered him to repay the debt. This he could not do and as the Brownsea clay had been suitable not for the finest porcelain but only terracotta and bricks it is doubtful if he was even able to maintain payments on the interest. Waugh fled to Spain and in 1857 the island was offered for auction as part of his bankruptcy proceedings but failed to reach its reserve price of £50,000 and was handed over to the bank. The following newspaper advertisement was published in 1869 and referred to the island by its old name:

> BRANKSEA POTTERY AND CLAY WORKS, NEAR POOLE, DORSET. The clay obtained from the pits on the island of BRANKSEA is of the finest quality, and the goods are manufactured with the aid of powerful machinery. The articles offered for sale will be found to bear comparison with the best goods manufactured in any part of England. Every article for drainage purposes may be had. List of Prices forwarded on application to ...
>
> RICHARD PETTS, MANAGER

Pottery Pier ['New Pier' on the 1857 map on the next page] **at the western extremity of Brownsea Island. St. Michael's Mount is the hill to the right. This shot is from the south, the waters of White Ground Lake between Brownsea Island and Furzey Island.**

Photographs: Colin Graham

Pottery Pier from the south-east, from the foot of St. Michael's Mount, looking along a beach that is strewn with the debris of the coarse-ware industry of 1853-87. Today's chimneys, on the skyline, are at Hamworthy power station which has dominated the harbour skyline since 1950.

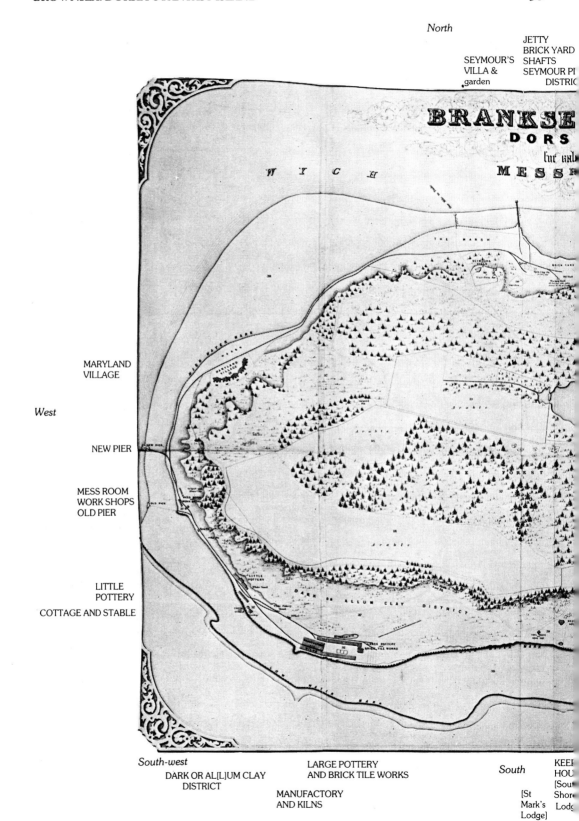

MESSRS. DRIVER'S MAP FOR THE 1857 SALE

East of centre
HOT HOUSES [Vinery] & KITCHEN GARDEN
THE WILDERNESS

North-east of centre
VILLA
THE PHEASANTRY

LAKES

North-east

ST ANDREW'S BAY LAND
(Arable and Pasture)
north
south

East

CHURCH
COASTGUARD STATION
QUAY

CASTLE

FARM BUILDINGS

HILL
BATTERY

South-east

TAGE
GARDEN

WHITE BRICK & TERRA COTTA CLAY DISTRICT
HICHCOCK'S
BRICK & TILE YARD   THE DEER PARK & Pasture

BARNES BRICK YARD

Survivals of old Brownsea. [Above] **A cottage, believed to be the oldest building on the Quay.**
Photographs: Colin Graham

An old claypit – one of the flooded workings beside Seymer's Marsh. This is towards the western side of the northern shore.

Seymer's House ('Seymour's Villa' on the 1857 map) overlooks the northern cliffs. Its ruins are entangled in the nature reserve established by Dorset Naturalists' Trust (renamed the Dorset Trust for Nature Conservation in 1986).

Photographs: Colin Graham

Only the walls stand of the hot-houses beside the island's former kitchen garden, south of the main path to the east of the centre of the island. There was in Victorian times a long expanse of south-facing glass, entangled with grapes and known as The Vinery.

Lesser, ornamental, walling near the island's main path. Undergrowth hides traces of a pheasantry. There was a deer park, in the south-east corner of the island next to Battery Hill.

VICTORIAN RELICS

The Coast Guard Station was completed in 1842 and stands between the Castle and the Quay. It had its own slipway.

Photographs: Colin Graham

There is a Victorian dovecote in the grounds of Brownsea Castle.

In 1870 Brownsea Island was sold to George Augustus Frederick Cavendish-Bentinck for £30,000. He took over Waugh's investment and continued the pottery industry until 1887. But the business was being run down and its working force declined from three hundred to only a hundred men at the close.

Summary of the prospectus and articles of association of the Branksea Island Company formed by Augustus Cavendish-Bentinck MP on 9 May 1873.
Courtesy: National Trust

THE BRANKSEA ISLAND COMPANY (LIMITED).

Capital Twenty Thousand Pounds in 2,000 Shares at £10 each. One Hundred Shares not allotted.

R. H. FRY, Manager.

LIST OF SHAREHOLDERS.

Right Hon. G. A. F. CAVENDISH BENTINCK, M.P.
WILLIAM GEORGE CAVENDISH BENTINCK, ESQ.
Sir HENRY DRUMMOND WOLFF, K.C.M.G., M.P.
Representatives of ALFRED SEYMOUR, Esq.
Representatives of Mrs. JANE WILD.
WILLIAM BURNYEAT, Esq.
RICHARD HENRY FRY, Esq.
WILLIAM GEORGE FREDERICK CAVENDISH BENTINCK, Esq.

This company was formed on the 9th of May, 1873, for the manufacture and sale of Pottery connected with sanitary works. And also for terra cotta work, such as chimney pots, ornamental figures, &c.

These works were commenced by Colonel Waugh, who put up the Pottery, Workmen's Cottages, and constructed the Tram Way round the north of the Island.

The following is a copy of the Memorandum of the Association :—

1st.—The name of the Company is "The Branksea Island Company Limited."

2nd.—The Registered Office of the Company will be situate in England.

3rd.—The objects for which the Company is established are—The manufacture of and dealing in pottery ware, bricks, tiles, drain-pipes and other pipes, chimney pots, terra-cotta, cement, alum and earthenware; and all articles composed or manufactured in whole or in part of clay, terra cotta or other earth; the sinking and digging for and raising and dealing in clay, earth, stone, coal, sand, and minerals, and other substances of a like nature; the carrying on for profit or gain of the businesses of bankers, merchants, builders, contractors, general dealers, shipbuilders, engineers, hotel keepers and licensed victuallers, ship owners and fishery proprietors, and the breeding, cultivating, seeking for, purchasing and selling oysters, spawn, fry, and fish of all descriptions; the carrying on, conducting, managing, and prosecuting of the said trades, or businesses, or any of them, in such manner and at such place or places, either in England or elsewhere, as the Company may think requisite or necessary, and either alone or in connection with any other trade, business, or commercial operation, which may be incident or ancillary or conducive to the objects aforesaid or any of them, and whether on account of the Company alone, or with or for any other Companies or persons; and the purchasing, taking in exchange or on lease, renting, or otherwise acquiring, holding, occupying, demising, employing, and managing, for any of the purposes or objects aforesaid, of any lands, buildings, hereditaments, structures, machinery, patents, licences to use patents, rights, easements, goods, chattles and effects, and other real and personal property, which in the opinion of the Company may be necessary or convenient for or ancillary to the carrying on of such trades or businesses, or any of them; the purchasing or acquisition of the property and goodwill of or any interest in any similar business, the promoting, financing, and taking shares in any Company or partnership, and the amalgamating in whole or in part with any Company or partnership carrying on business similar to the business of this Company; the selling, granting, mortgaging or otherwise disposing of any of the property of the Company; the entering into and accepting of all such contracts, agreements and leases, and the making of all such arrangements, and the doing of all such other things as are incidental or conducive to the attainment of the above objects.

4th.—The Liability of the Members is limited.

5th.—The Capital of the Company is £20,000, divided into 2000 Shares of £10 each.

Above. **Pottery Pier, at the western extremity of the island, was the 'New Pier' of 1853. The old one was two hundred yards to the south.**
Photograph: Colin Graham

Opposite. **In 1881 the Branksea Pottery, trading as the Branksea Island Company since 1873, obtained testimonials for its sewer pipes – not quite the fine porcelain that Colonel and Mrs Waugh visualised they would be manufacturing. Even the sanitary engineers would fail to save the business and it finally folded in 1887.**
Courtesy: National Trust

Below. **The overgrown site of Brownsea's industrial heartland – the potteries were at the side of Lincoln Cliff in the south-west corner of the island.**
Photograph: Colin Graham

THE BRANKSEA ISLAND CO., LIMITED.

(LATE BRANKSEA POTTERY.)

First and only Prize awarded by Sanitary Institute of Great Britain.

MANUFACTURERS OF BEST

SALT-GLAZED STONEWARE, DRAIN PIPES, SYPHONS, GULLIES, TRAPS, INVERTS, TERRA COTTA CHIMNEY POTS AND CHIMNEY CORES, FIRE BRICKS, GARDEN EDGINGS, ETC., ETC.

BRISTOL WARE CLAY, FIRE CLAY, AND DRAIN PIPE CLAY.

PRICE AND QUALITY CANNOT BE SURPASSED BY ANY FIRM IN THE COUNTY.

VESSELS LOADED ALONGSIDE.

Price List on application. R. H. FRY, Managing Director.

WORKS: BRANKSEA, POOLE, DORSET.

TESTIMONIALS.

From the Urban Sanitary Authority, Surveyor's Office, Town Hall, Basingstoke,
August 14th, 1881.

Dear Sir,—In accordance with the request contained in your letter of yesterday, I have much pleasure in informing you that when the drainage of this town was decided on, various manufacturers of pipes were invited to send samples of their pipes for testing purposes. Many samples were accordingly sent, and tested under my supervision; three samples were selected as answering to the terms of the Specification; among these were yours, which were found to be the strongest of all; these when broken were found to be of a close grained material, free from shakes and grits, in fact having the appearance of being of an imperishable nature; after soaking in water for several hours I found the quantity of water absorbed very small indeed. The pipes were well moulded, strongly socketed, and their strength to resist bursting or crushing is very considerable.

All the Sewers laid here, about seven miles, are laid with your pipes, a large portion being under great pressure, the Valley Line being about four feet under water, and some of the cuttings being about twenty feet deep.

I have also laid your pipes in other places, and after considerable experience my opinion is that they are some of the STRONGEST and best pipes for Sanitary purposes manufactured.

I am, yours truly, S. WESTCOTT, Borough Surveyor.
To R. H. Fry, Esq., Manager, Branksea Island Company, Limited, Poole.

From W. P. Winter and Son, Wholsale Drain Pipe, Slate, Cement, and Lias Lime Merchants, Blackfriars-road, Southsea, and Railway Station, Landport.—January 21st, 1880.

Dear Sir,—We have very much pleasure in stating that we have dealt with the Branksea Island Company over eight years, and for the last five years paying from three to four thousand pounds yearly, is quite sufficient guarantee of the quality of your goods being undeniable; having during the time above stated supplied under contract the Shanklin and West Cowes Local Boards (Isle of Wight) with your goods, which gave the greatest satisfaction

We have also obtained the contract for supplying the Local Board of Portsmouth for the THIRD time, which are now supplying, without having one complaint, as also our very large connection with the same result, at the same time being large users ourselves, with 30 years' experience, we are in a position to testify to the above.—Yours obediently,
To Mr. Fry, Branksea. W. P. WINTER AND SON.

I, James Patrick, hereby certify that I have this day, by order of Mr. R. H. FRY, (Manager of the Branksea Pottery), tested several 9-inch Drain Pipes to 140lbs. pressure to square inch.
(Signed) JAMES PATRICK, From Stone & Co., Engineers, Poole.
GEORGE MARKS, Pottery Timekeeper.

A 9-inch Drain Pipe has been tested to 240lbs. to square inch.

Maryland Village – the crescent of pottery workers' cottages built at the north-west corner of the island in 1855. They are seen in 1961, after wartime use as a flare decoy to draw German bombers, and the National Trust decided to finish the job of blowing them up.
Courtesy: National Trust

'Words could not picture its loveliness' – the vicar, 1881

Life on the island in late Victorian times, when it was an occasional summertime retreat for the Right Honourable George Augustus Frederick Cavendish-Bentinck, the Honourable Member for Whitehaven, was described by the vicar of Brownsea, Reverend Theophilus Bennett MA, in a vignette of 1881. 'A Sketch of Brownsea Island' attempts to convey the meaning of "My Island":

> It cannot always occur to a citizen that it means no catching of trains, no Vandemons, no school-boards or burglaries, no election fights, no insubordination, squalor, or poverty, but "My Island" signifies all this and much more.
>
> It signifies no police, because there is no need of police; no sanitation, because there is no dangers to life; no legislation, because there are no conflicting interests to legislate about; no rate assessing vestries, because there is nothing to rate at any one for; no business competition; nothing, in fact, that makes the hair prematurely grey, that furrows the forehead with lines, and ages men before their time. There is a whole gospel of truths in the two words, a gospel of peace and quiet, restfulness and comfort.
>
> The happy inhabitants of this island in the negative sense rise superior to the old world, which has to content itself with living on Continents, many millions of people side by side, and smothered up in bricks and mortar and conventionalism. They are fenced off from all intruders by an inviolable sea. And there is no need of walls or

palings, for old Father Neptune has girt it round with his own briny element.

First impressions are sometimes truest. And those that the first sight of this island gave me are scarcely translatable into words. I felt that human language failed to convey an adequate impression, that words could not picture its loveliness, and that it must be seen to be at all adequately appreciated.

Climate has much to do with health, and health with happiness. And here there is a climate so salubrious that the death rate is below that of the fabled "Hygeia."

The air is cool and refrigerating in summer, and mild and genial in winter. Exotics bloom in this favoured spot at Christmas; for here centre the perfections of Cannes, Mentone, and Algiers.

The scenery is undulating and picturesque, and very diversified. Suddenly you come upon a spacious chase of greensward, and next emerge upon an entrancing woodland scene, carpeted with feathery ferns, over which wave the ostrich-like plumes of the dark green pines. Next you see "Clear Lake" reflecting the Swiss Cottage and the Bridge of the Rialto. Stansfield has employed his pencil on the marine views, and there is still ample employment for his successors. A Mechi might delight himself in the agricultural arrangements, for all are the best of their kind.

"What man has done, man may do." Man has reclaimed thousands of acres from the vasty deep, and on this island he has succeeded in rescuing about one hundred acres, which he keeps dry by ingenious contrivances – such as perpetually revolving windmills, and other devices ...

... of which devices perhaps the most crucial was the abundance of human labour necessary to sustain the idyll. Bennett was fully aware of this as he carried out the listing of his flock for the 1881 national census.

CENSUS OF BROWNSEA ISLAND

Taken on Wednesday, 31st August, 1881, by Theophilus Bennett, M.A., Vicar.

	No. in family
Villa.—G. W. Cavendish-Bentinck, Esq., wife, and one daughter, Miss Venetia Cavendish-Bentinck, and eleven servants	15
Villino.—Rev. Theophilus Bennett, M.A., wife, and one servant	3
Manager's House.—R. H. Fry, Esq., wife, three sons, two daughters Governess, and one servant	9
Magazino.—George Gibson, wife, Miss M. Shirley	3
St. Mark's Cottage.—George Marks, wife, and one (girl) child	3
Pheasantry in Venetia Park.—J. Barnfield, wife, and W. R. Kennaway	3
" " —G. C. Tucker, wife, and one daughter	3

Turret.—T. Batterick and wife	2
Laundry.—L. Smith, wife, and A. Thumbwood	3
Farm Yard.—C. Old and wife	2
„ —J. Baker, wife, one son, and one daughter	4
„ —W. Doggett, wife, two sons and one daughter	5
Purbeck Cottage.—J. Payte, wife, and one grandchild	3
Semi-detached House.—J. Thirkettle, wife, two sons, and three daughters	7
Semi-detached House.—George Green, wife, and one daughter	3
Pottery.—J. Howard, wife. one son, and three daughters	6
—T. Summers, wife, one child, and F. Curtis	4
Seymour's Cottage.—D. Bates, wife, and C. White	3
Vinery.—C. Cobb, wife, and one daughter	3
„ J. Trevot, S. Holloway, and A. Gardiner	3
Maryland, 1.—*Island Inn and Store.*—Mr. G. Petts, wife, and two servants	4
„ 2.—W. Anstie, wife, one son, two daughters, and F. Froude	6
„ 3a.—R. Thomas, wife, one son, and two daughters	5
„ 3b.—C. Whitty, wife, one son, and H. Byles	4
„ 4.—J. Whittenham, wife, one son, two daughters, F. Lacey, R. Norris, F. Hoar, and W. Gillingham	9
„ 5.—J. Whittenham, wife, two sons, W. Singleton, J. Thomas, and J. Dunford	7
„ 6.—E. Burgess, wife, four sons, and two daughters	8
„ 7.—J. C. Parker, wife, and three daughters	5
„ 8.—W. Whittenham, wife, T. Biggs, wife, J. Welsh and wife	6
„ 9a.—L. World and wife	2
„ 9b.- T. Deane, wife, and one daughter	3
„ 10.—S. W. Teague, wife, two sons, one daughter, G. Upwood, J. Potter, and F. Jones	8
„ 11a.—S. Hordle, wife, and one daughter	3

„	11b.—F. Vincent, wife, and one child		3
„	12a.—A. Real, wife, and S. Hooper		3
„	12b.—J. Churchill, wife, and one son		3
„	13.—W. Real, wife, J. Cheeseman, C. Britt, and E Hibbs		5
„	14.—B. Palmer, wife, four sons, and H. Biggs		7
„	15.—E. Gray, wife, and one grandchild		3
„	16.—J. Eyles, wife, W. Kelley, wife, F. Temperlin, and C. Hawley		6
„	17.—*Infant School.*—B. Byles and wife		2
„	18.—A. Real, wife, one son, one daughter, J. Leslie, and H. Jackson		6
„	19.—H. Tucker, wife, three sons, two daughters, E. J. Tucker, and A. Tucker		9
The Cassino, 1a.—J. Old, wife, one son, and one daughter			4
„ 1b.—J. Foot, wife, two sons, and one daughter			5
Piazza del Castello, 2.—C. Old, wife, one son, and one daughter			4
„	„	3.—D. Rolf, wife, two sons, and two daughters	6
„	„	4.—J. Stockley, wife, M. J. Froude	3
„	„	5.—R. Stockley, wife, and one daughter	3
„	„	6.—J. Moody, wife, and two sons	5
„	„	7.—W. Deane, wife, four sons, and two daughters	8
„	„	8.—G. Sansom, wife, two sons, and two daughters	6
„	„	9.—H. Carter, wife, and two daughters	4
,	„	10.—Three Stable Helpers	3
„	„	11.—S. Wareham, wife, two sons, and one daughter	5
„	„	12.—J. Laurence, wife, one son, one daughter	4
„	„	13.—G. Burgess, wife, three sons, and one daughter	6

Population 270.

Cavendish-Bentinck dies, 1891

Cavendish-Bentinck brought to Brownsea numerous objets d'art from southern Europe including a fifteenth century Italian classical well-head, a pozzo, of faded pink marble. After 9 April 1891 it served as his gravestone and a wrought iron plaque was added to commemorate his reign. Five years later his widow, Prudence, died and a second plate was added.

An elegant Italian marble pozzo, with the crest of the Leza family, which dates from 1497 and is set in Brownsea's churchyard as a memorial:

'BENEATH THIS SPOT RESTS THE BODY
OF THE RIGHT HONOURABLE
GEORGE AUGUSTUS FREDERICK
CAVENDISH-BENTINCK
OF HER MAJESTY'S PRIVY COUNCIL
AND MEMBER OF PARLIAMENT
IN WHICH HE SAT FOR 31 CONSECUTIVE YEARS
BORN JULY 9 1821   DIED APRIL 9 1891
ONLY SON OF MAJOR GENERAL LORD FREDERICK
CAVENDISH-BENTINCK
AND GRANDSON OF WILLIAM HENRY
THIRD DUKE OF PORTLAND.'

'ALSO IN MEMORY
OF
PRUDENCE PENELOPE WIDOW OF THE LATE
RT HON[BLE] GEORGE AUGUSTUS
CAVENDISH-BENTINCK.
SECOND DAUGHTER
OF
COL. POWELL LESLIE
OF GLASSLOUGH, Co. MONAGHAN
IRELAND
BORN NOVEMBER 8 1828
DIED JUNE 22 1896.'

Fire guts the Castle, 1896

The island had been sold to another MP, Kenneth Robert Balfour, who would stand helplessly watching the contents of his island mansion being consumed by fire. He had been at prayer, for evensong, as it gained a hold and the islanders were unable to fight the subsequent inferno. Not for the last time that night, of 26 January 1896, Brownsea provided a spectacle for the mainlanders.

Restoration in 1897 was to soften the castle's lines and remove some of the turrets and other extremities of the gothic flourishes. For Balfour, however, there was another impending tragedy. His wife's health was worsening after years of chronic illness and he put the island up for auction, at The Mart, by the Bank of England, on 13 July 1899. Margaret Anne was to die on 23 March 1901.

From 1900, Balfour represented Bournemouth in Parliament; elected on a promise to "Maintain intact our Imperial heritage" – "no home rule for Ireland; no 'godless' education for our children; no disestablishment of the Church of England; no weakening of our defensive forces ..."

Branksea's name becomes Brownsea, 1903

Kenneth Balfour was succeeded on Brownsea in 1901 by a wealthy socialite from the same political camp. Charles van Raalte nearly became Balfour's next-door neighbour in Parliament but as the Unionist [Tory] candidate for East Dorset he failed to swing Poole's traditional Liberal loyalties. He used the island to entertain numerous guests and maintained a band of twenty uniformed musicians who played in the summer evenings on the castle lawn and then in the great hall of the castle during winter. It is a pity van Raalte changed the name of Branksea to Brownsea in 1903, though if you lived on an island and your guests kept getting out at Branksome Station by mistake you'd soon come to the same decision.

Photograph opposite: Colin Graham.
Drawing: David Murdock
Picture: Rodney Legg collection

Owner [right] **Charles van Raalte and the visitor who was to bring his island its lasting fame** [above]: **Robert Baden Powell.**

Baden-Powell and world's first scout camp, 1907

Of all those who came to Brownsea the one whose memory has been most lasting was Robert Baden-Powell, in 1907. He lived out his life in the false glory of the charade that had happened in the little Kalahari township of Mafeking. He went against orders, wrote himself a credit note for £500,000, and allowed himself to be holed-up in the place of least strategic importance in the whole of South Africa. He had tricked the Cape Government into allowing him to take some guards into Mafeking to protect stores and used this as an excuse to move his whole regiment into a place where, as he knew, they would be surrounded. Others fought and won the Boer War while Baden-Powell revelled in luxury, dressing up in outlandish clothes, playing polo and writing: "Everything in the garden is lovely." Seldom was a Boer seen and only four white civilians were killed in the entire 'siege'. When the relief column finally entered the town it was given little attention and the commanding officer of an advance patrol told a bystander who he was and what it meant. "Oh yes, I heard you were knocking about," the man replied. One of the officers of the relief column remarked of the relieved: "I have never known men so sulky, or march with such bad grace." Even though the nation went mad after the news "Relief of Mafeking" arrived at Reuter's Fleet Street office at 9.17 p.m. on 18 May 1900, the War Office did not forgive the man who had prevented 1,200 armed men from fighting in the war and there were no special military honours for Baden-Powell. He was the emptiest hero the nation had ever adopted and the myth of Mafeking was written as if it were one of the greatest happenings in our history.

Baden-Powell's lasting contribution to the world started on Brownsea between 1-9 August 1907 when he held a camp for about twenty boys on the south-west side of the island. For ten days they were divided into four patrols, taught games and treated as unarmed boy soldiers. A scout, in B-P's words, was: "Trusty, loyal, helpful, brotherly, courteous, kind, obedient, smiling, thrifty, pure as the rustling wind." It is difficult to visualise how the world-wide scouting movement could have grown from such a beginning. Only Baden-Powell with his quick-witted and obstinate driving power, together with an undeserved place in the nation's heart, could have made the idea work.

Beaters and pheasants, bagged by one of Charles van Raalte's shooting parties, about 1905.

Tea party given at Brownsea Castle by Charles and Florence van Raalte for the island staff.

House party guests at Brownsea Castle, about 1905. Front row – Charles van Raalte, Nonny, Margot and Babs (with her Pomeranian). Centre row – Mrs Charteris, Florence van Raalte, Lady Howard de Walden and Dick Charteris. Back row – Lord Ludlow, Pendrode Zuleuta, Ralph Dickson and Lord Norbury.

Photographs: from 'Brownsea Islander' edited by Gail Lawson for Jack Battrick

Henrietta Dunn and the Brownsea schoolchildren early in the twentieth century.
Courtesy: National Trust

Garden Staff, just after lunch on a warm summer day in the 1890s. The conservatories are gone.

Brownsea Castle, from its lawn and the private beach, in 1985.
Photographs: Colin Graham

Above. **The van Raaltes' drawing room in Brownsea Castle.** [Opposite]. **The Battery, in an Edwardian water colour by Florence van Raalte, and her dining room at Brownsea Castle**
Source: Rodney Legg collection

Charles van Raalte fought and lost two elections for the Unionist Party in the East Dorset Parliamentary constituency, which included the town of Poole. The Unionists were the predecessors of the present Conservatives, the Conservative and Unionist Party finally abandoning the word in the early 1970s to distance itself from Ulster fanaticism.

Van Raalte's defeats have to be seen against a background of Poole's traditional liberalism. He was fighting against the tide as the Liberals took the country and Chancellor of the Exchequer David Lloyd George was to impose supertax at the rate of 6d in the pound (2½%) to help finance a social security programme. Charles van Raalte was depressed and went on holiday to India, in 1907, but he caught pneumonia and died in Calcutta. His embalmed body was shipped home for burial on the island and his widow, Florence, stayed in residence at the Castle.

COLLECTIONS OF TREASURES

Below. **Just a part of Charles van Raalte's collection of musical instruments in Brownsea Castle.**
Source: Rodney Legg collection

Opposite. **The billiard room at Brownsea Castle and the greatest art treasure in the house, the fine old tapestry panel 'Winter' by French dyers Gilles and Jehan Gobelin which was to make 3,500 guineas when the castle contents were sold in 1927. It was made in about 1450.**
Source: Rodney Legg collection

Florence van Raalte's death ends an era

The island's Edwardian gentleman, Charles van Raalte, had exuded refinement and privilege. His widow, Florence, was if anything too kind on the islanders. Their lives remained immune from the upheavals of war and the crushing despair of peace. The rest of the nation was adapting to gradual change, that had been transforming society since the 1860s. Then, for the first time, the number of people in manufacturing industry outnumbered those in domestic service. Brownsea's community in the 1920s was a living fossil, drawing all its sustenance from an owner's investment beyond its shores – and such incomes were not going to survive the decade intact.

In the event, Florence died before the slump. Brownsea's fate, in 1927, was to fall into the hands of a dictator – a lady with a name that sounds like a merger between two West End auction rooms.

The memorial chapel added to the south side of the tower of St Mary's church in 1908. Charles van Raalte had died in 1907, and was brought back from India, but his devoted Florence would not join him till 1927:

'IN
BONAM MEMORIAM
CAROLI van RAALTE
DE INSVLA BROWNSEA QVINATVS
AD MDCCCLVII [Born 1857].
OBIIT AD MCMVII [Died 1907].
HOC MONVMENTVM POSVIT CONJVX
EJVX DEVOTISSIMA FLORENTIA.'

Photograph: Colin Graham

Plan to 'dismantle the Castle', 1927

Meanwhile, however, between the ownership of the van Raaltes and the coming of Mrs Christie, Brownsea had the shortest of interim regimes at the hands of a house clearer. Though he only owned the island for a matter of months, Sir Arthur Wheeler "decided, in view of probable future developments on the island, to dismantle the castle". He instructed Fox and Sons to auction every removable

Freeland and Hannah Battrick, who had farmed Brownsea, beside the Quay Cottages. They were evicted from the island in 1927.
Photograph: from 'Brownsea Islander' edited by Gail Lawson for Jack Battrick (their son)

object, including the furnishings of its thirty-eight bedrooms and a 5,000 volume library, which were sold over nine days between 13 and 23 June 1927.

All the property, it was emphasised, was that of the van Raaltes. The auctioneers denied rumours that the odd additional treasure had been shipped across to take advantage of the considerable interest and expected high prices. A shuttle service of little boats would be required to deposit all the island's trappings back on the quayside at Sandbanks.

The 156-page catalogue had 2,714 lots and many of these were for multiple items. There were collections of musical instruments, arms and armour, marbles and other statuary, and paintings and tapestries. A fine old Gobelin panel, 'Winter', from about 1450, made 3,500 guineas. It had been illustrated by Country Life as a choice example of the weavers' art.

The sale realised a total of £22,300 but was not to be followed by the proposed demolition of the castle.

Brownsea's Battrick family on the island Quay at the eve of the evictions, 1929. Depopulation started the Christie regime, at a time of national austerity and recession when post-war economics extinguished the embers of Victorian and Edwardian lifestyles. The elderly couple, Hannah and Freeland Battrick, were the island's retired farmers. Between them sit daughter Dorothy and son Jack. Immediately behind them, the island's boat clung to the past with its name – 'BRANKSEA' rather than the usurping Brownsea. This is another of the evocative pictures from 'Brownsea Islander': Jack's story which Gail Lawson recorded with subtle and sympathetic ghosting shortly before he died. It was published by Poole Historical Trust.

NINE DAYS' SALE

BROWNSEA CASTLE
BROWNSEA ISLAND - POOLE HARBOUR - DORSET

Five minutes by Motor Boat from Sandbanks Pier, four miles from Bournemouth
(for means of access, see General Remarks)

CATALOGUE
OF THE

Contents *of the* Mansion

including

APPOINTMENTS OF 38 BEDROOMS

DRAWING ROOM, MUSIC ROOM, BILLIARD ROOM
DINING ROOM, STUDY, GRAND HALL & GALLERY

Valuable Persian, Indian and Turkey Carpets. English and French Furniture. Three Pianofortes, Steck Pianola, Player-Piano, American Organ. Billiard Table

Valuable Collection of Musical Instruments
formed by the late C. Van Raalte, Esq.

Decorative China and Porcelain. Ornamental items and Bronzes.
Coloured and other Engravings. Water Colours.

COLLECTION OF OIL PAINTINGS

Four Suits of Armour. Arms and Weapons.

THIRTEEN PANELS OF FRENCH AND BRUSSELS TAPESTRY
and
LIBRARY OF ABOUT 5,000 VOLUMES

which

Messrs. FOX & SONS

Are favoured with instructions from Sir Arthur Wheeler, Bt., to Sell by Auction, on the premises, as above, on

MONDAY to FRIDAY (inclusive) JUNE 13, 14, 15, 16 & 17, 1927
and
MONDAY to THURSDAY (inclusive) JUNE 20, 21, 22 & 23, 1927
commencing each day at **12.30** precisely

ON VIEW, by catalogues only, Tuesday, Wednesday, Thursday and Friday, June 7th to 10th, 1927, from 10 to 5 o'clock each day

Illustrated Catalogues (complete 7/6) or Sections: Furniture and General Effects, 2/6; Pictures and Tapestries, 2/6; Books, 2/6; Musical Instruments and Armour, 2/6; may be obtained of the AUCTIONEERS, 44-50, OLD CHRISTCHURCH RD., BOURNEMOUTH

The timetable for the clearance sale of the entire contents of Brownsea Castle, carried out by Bournemouth auctioneers Fox and Sons – 2,715 lots spread over nine days in the midsummer of 1927.

Source: Rodney Legg collection

ORDER OF SALE

First Day. Monday, June 13th, 1927   LOTS
commencing at 12.30 p.m. precisely
Bedrooms Nos. 1 to 16 and Workroom   ...   1 to 319

Second Day. Tuesday, June 14th, 1927
commencing at 12.30 p.m. precisely
Bedrooms Nos. 17 to 24   ...   .   320 to 588

Third Day. Wednesday, June 15th, 1927
commencing at 12.30 p.m. precisely
Bedrooms Nos. 25 to 30, Principal Staircase and
Gallery, and Study   ...   .   589 to 832

Fourth Day. Thursday, June 16th, 1927
commencing at 12.30 p.m. precisely
Coloured Engravings and Prints, Tapestries and
Needlework, Oil & Water Colour Paintings   833 to 1066

Fifth Day. Friday, June 17th, 1927
commencing at 12.30 p.m. precisely
Drawing Room, Music Room and Billiard Room 1067 to 1339

Sixth Day. Monday, June 20th, 1927
commencing at 12.30 p.m. precisely
The Extensive Library of Books   ...   ... 1340 to 1720

Seventh Day. Tuesday, June 21st, 1927
commencing at 12.30 p.m. precisely
Musical Instruments and Armour and Arms   ... 1721 to 2038

Eighth Day. Wednesday, June 22nd, 1927
commencing at 12.30 p.m. precisely
Grand Hall, Dining Room and Silver and Plate 2039 to 2373

Ninth Day. Thursday, June 23rd, 1927
commencing at 12.30 p.m. precisely
Statuary, Contents of Bathing Houses, Wines,
Garden Floor Rooms, China, Glass & Offices 2374 to 2715

Mrs Bonham Christie arrives in 1927 and evicts the islanders

Mrs Mary Florence Bonham Christie bought the island in 1927 for £125,000 and gradually sealed it off from the world, ending a way of life for its islanders.

Jack Battrick was born on Brownsea Island in September 1909, in a terraced farm cottage overlooking the Home Field. In 1929 he was evicted from the island along with his family and just about all its domestics and estate staff. Mrs Bonham Christie took an immediate decision to do without its dozens of servants. Then, or very soon afterwards, she also decided to cease gardening the island, and let it return to nature.

Visitor thrown in the sea, 1933

Mrs Bonham Christie once relented to pressure in 1932, and allowed five hundred scouts to invade the island for their jubilee celebrations. This was too much for her and in 1933 she accosted a bait-digger on the beach and said: "If you come here again my servants have orders to throw you, and anybody belonging to you, in the sea." He did return and the warning was carried out by a Scandinavian lady, Bertha Horthung Olsen, who threw his daughter into the sea. A disastrous fire in 1934 killed most of the wildlife and left the island badly scarred for the next twenty years; its damage can even be seen today where dead trees stand amongst the revived woodlands. The flames raged for three days and only a change of wind saved the buildings at the eastern end of the island from destruction; immense columns of smoke became dense clouds that were carried across the Channel and over to France.

Billowing clouds of smoke at the start of the great fire of Brownsea Island, photographed by Benjamin Pond at 8.30 in the morning. By nightfall the northern shore was a raging furnace. Hundreds worked the following day to try and stop its spread but they could do little more than save the furniture from a cottage – and that had to be taken back up the beach as the tide advanced. The smoke by now was trailing across the Channel to France and the newsmen had arrived from London. On the third day the unemployed from Poole were ferried across to smash a clearing and a token trench across the island. The flames were set to jump it but in the afternoon the wind changed direction and the eastern end of the island, with all the important buildings, was spared. In the peat bogs the fire continued to smoulder for weeks. Gossip in Poole claimed arson and blamed a disgruntled poacher who was said to have rowed across from Poole to the Maryland shore early that morning.

Mrs Christie's attempts to keep the island undisturbed then became totally determined and even the naturalist Peter Scott was later banned as an undesirable. Creating a forbidden land caused mystery that appealed to the outside world. Mrs Christie spent her life in just one of the castle's many rooms and was surrounded by crates with many of her possessions that were never unpacked. Outside the castle stood two old vehicles that had not been used for years: a Morris car and a Ford lorry. Early in 1940 there were rumours in Poole that the island was being used by a German espionage network. Our own soldiers were later billeted on the island, ate many of the peacocks, and generally decimated the island's animals and birds.

Armada of Aliens

Crowds of visitors were to pass through the island. The Navy shepherded an armada of small Dutch craft down the English Channel to Brownsea after the Nazis had smashed into the Low Countries – bringing down the Chamberlain government in the process – on 10 May 1940. Three thousand refugees were herded on to Brownsea and all had to be given security clearance before being allowed any further. "Ideally suited for the purpose", commented Victor W. Swatridge who had been a Divisional Aliens Officer for Dorset Police.

Guns return to Battery Hill

The island's ancient Battery Hill – so called from the days of cannon – was chosen, just south-west from the castle, as a mounting point for two six-inch naval guns, to guard the mouth of Poole Harbour. These guns were manned by 110 men from 347 Coast Battery of the Royal Artillery and were operative from 1940. The harbour entrance was sealed at night and guarded by an Examination Ship, minefields, Navy patrol boats and old ships packed with explosives that were ready if necessary for blocking the Main Channel.

Brownsea lured the German bombs, 1941-44

Early in 1941 an MSND [Major Strategic Night Decoy] had been established at the western end of Brownsea Island, with flares to draw bombers from Poole and Bournemouth. It was operated by RAF personnel in a bunker about five hundred feet from the flares. Lawrence Popplewell, writing in issue thirty-five of Dorset County Magazine described the rows of large wire baskets, courtesy of the pyrotechnics department at Elstree Studios, packed with shavings and soaked in paraffin, fired electrically from the bunker, to simulate rows of burning buildings: "By far the most ingenious method, however, was that which gave the effect of bombs bursting. This, on Brownsea, took the form of a bath tub and two lavatory cisterns. The bath contained wood and coal, again ignited electrically from the shelter, and then the cisterns were pulled and emptied alternately. One fed the fire with flushes of paraffin which gave a rapid spurt of flame. The other then added the master touch by flushing water which produced a white hot flash, exactly like a bomb bursting, especially when seen from the air."

This was especially effective in the early hours of 22 May 1942 when radar tracked a force of enemy bombers from the Pas de Calais down the Channel to St Catherine's Point on the Isle of Wight where they turned north-westwards, directly for Poole. A pathfinder dropped incendiaries on the town to guide the fifty-five bombers. These were brought under control in time for the Brownsea unit to unleash its alternative fireworks and for twenty minutes the west end of the island rocked with countless explosions. In all its wartime career was to save Poole and Bournemouth from a thousand tons of German bombs.

Treasury gives island to National Trust, 1962

The island's history of eccentricity ended with Mrs Christie's death in her ninety-eighth year, on 28 April 1961, and her grandson, John Bonham Christie, presented the island to the Treasury in lieu of death duties. The Government handed it to the National Trust in 1962. When the visitors came, a wide area at the west of the island was swept by fire in 1963 and there were fears of a repetition of 1934 when the flames spread across virtually the entire island. Firebreaks were cut and a fire watching and fighting system established: with the island attracting so many (93,282 people landed in 1971) the wilderness became endangered each summer and had to be closed whilst south Dorset burnt in the drought of 1976.

Jack Battrick, one of the islanders evicted by Mrs Bonham Christie, returned to Brownsea to work for the National Trust in the pacification of its

Ruins of Maryland, the village constructed for pottery workers in 1855 above the north-western shore – the opposite end of the island from the Castle. There were twenty terraced cottages, set in a crescent looking out to sea. They were roofless when the National Trust had them blown up in 1963. Here a copper is still intact in the corner of a scullery.

Photograph: Colin Graham

jungle. He told his story to Gail Lawson who ghosted it in subtle and sympathetic fashion for 'Brownsea Islander' which was published by Poole Historical Trust. Jack sadly never saw his book in print, as he died on 25 February 1978 and was buried at Brownsea on 3 March.

How National Trust members heard that Her Majesty's Treasury had given them Brownsea.

NEWS LETTER

Spring 1963

ANNUAL GENERAL MEETING

The 1962 Annual General Meeting was held on Friday 12th October at the Fishmongers Hall, by kind permission of the Court of Assistants.

In the absence of Lord Crawford, who was unwell and unable to attend, Lord Rosse presided.

Of the transfer of Brownsea Island by the Treasury, working through the Land Fund, he said: 'This is only one of several important properties that have already come to the Trust through this medium. It is a medium that is working extremely well and is a magnificent tribute to the former Chancellor, Lord Dalton, whose conception it was.'

BROWNSEA ISLAND, DORSET

The Island will be open to the public from 16th May, a date fixed as early as possible, despite the certainty that much work needed to receive visitors will not be completed. What will a visitor find to do?

The Island is essentially an unspoiled heathland set in the midst of Poole Harbour, its back on the urban development of Poole and Sandbanks, facing into the sunshine and beauty of the Isle of Purbeck. Enjoyment in the main must be derived from walking, picnicing and bathing in such surroundings. Part of the Island will be kept secluded as a reserve for wild life – principally birds – and later on it will be possible for those interested to go on special visits to see them. The wild peacocks will, we hope, not be too shy to display themselves.

The Church has much charm and interest and will, no doubt, be a focal centre.

The Castle, however, despite its impressive bulk has little antiquity or architectural interest, and will not be open.

Those who come to the Island will find peace and beauty – unless they themselves destroy it.

Baden-Powell's cottage, ruined on the southern shore, at the time of the 1961 press visit.
Courtesy: Evening Echo, Bournemouth

The 1961 media visit

The next casualty after Mrs Christie's death was Brownsea's extravagent folklore. In May 1961 the first media visitors to the forbidden land failed to find a single giant rat from the hoards that she was said to have gone out and fed at midnight. Neither did they find the tropical rain forest, or the German spies still in hiding from the Second World War. The last line in Poole stories was an absurdity given that the island had been occupied by the Royal Artillery and turned into a decoy to attract German bombers. About all the pressmen discovered were a few hungry mosquitoes.

They made much of the iron curtain that was said to have descended across the harbour and cut off a Shangri-la. It was news that someone might have landed and built a sandcastle. Stories then inevitably turned to Robinson Crusoe, and the bearded pipe-smoking protector of Brownsea's wildlife, "the Bird Man of Brownsea", Vere Capel, was there to oblige. He had arrived in 1959. The peacocks were nervous of the photographers and refused to pose but at meal-time they flocked on to the lawn for the garish appearance of Vere Capel in his yellow coat.

Mrs Bonham Christie, the wife of grandson John, carried out a public relations exercise on behalf of old Mrs Christie, the mystic chatelaine of Brownsea. The reporters expressed shock that the little cottage opposite Furzey Island on the mid southern shore, where Baden-Powell had stayed in 1907, was now a roofless ruin. "Of course the cottages were left derelict," Mrs Bonham Christie explained. "They were bombed during the war. There was no point rebuilding them, for there was no one to live in them. But the sea-wall and castle were beautifully preserved. She looked after the essentials."

Not that life was quite as detached as Poole people pretended. The postman had landed every morning at eight o'clock to open the Victorian letter-box even though there might not be anything inside. There was, however, no telephone – which showed that Mrs Christie had some sense. "One of the joys of the place," Mrs Bonham Christie was now finding.

Time had literally not been stilled on Brownsea as the clock was still wound each day, even if the 150 peacocks were the only inhabitants who were much fussed about the time. Yet the story demanded a time-warp and the reporters were relieved to discover Mrs Christie's car, a Bullnose Morris, which had been kept in running order. The new Bonham Christies were quite taken with it, and would in fact do just that. "You won't see one like that in England," John's wife told the press and obligingly hesitated. "I mean, the mainland."

The car was to disappear but I was to track it down later in the story. By then it was in danger of visiting a mainland scrapyard.

Alan Bromby takes over, 1962

The National Trust appointed an all-purpose 39-year-old man of the islands as its head warden. Alan Bromby had fought in the Navy during the war and gone to work for Lady Iliffe [Charlotte Gilding, died 1972] on Furzey Island in 1948. He was there for ten years and then wardened Round Island for S. L. Fowler. That island was sold in 1961 and Alan Bromby, by now a skilled boatman who was as familiar as any with the island waters, was the obvious choice for the National Trust's main job.

They gave him a tractor so that he could reinstate the paths into the overgrown hinterland. Alan and Joan Bromby were set to run Brownsea for the next three decades.

Alan Bromby beside the Quay at Brownsea on his appointment as the island's head warden, 1962.
Courtesy: Southern Newspapers

'Maryland. This seat was donated to commemorate the site of the home of the Toms family.'
Photograph: Colin Graham

Maryland Village, demolished in 1963

The National Trust occupation begins as a relief beyond question, but one could be asked. A picture in Jack's book shows the long crescent shaped grouping of five terraces – each of four pottery workers' cottages – at Maryland Village in the north-west corner of the island. Their roofs are collapsed but the walls and chimneys are solid enough. The caption records their end in 1963: "Maryland in the 1960s. Bombing, neglect and fire had ravaged the village and the dangerous ruins were cleared before the island was opened to visitors."

That was the standard answer to the problem of old buildings in the 1960s. If they had been wired off and left till today, the Landmark Trust might have rescued them for holiday lets, as it does with the cottages on Lundy Island, but on Brownsea, perhaps rightly the animals and birds had the priority.

Squirrels, hedgehogs, herons and terns

Of particular importance amongst Brownsea's wildlife is its colony of our native red squirrel. The grey species spread across Dorset in the ten years after the last war and the red squirrel was eliminated almost everywhere. But the greys were not introduced to Brownsea and the island is now one of the last safe refuges of the red squirrel in southern England. They are especially common in Beech Valley on the island. Disease was the one threat they seemed to be facing in the 1960s though the population seems now to be stable, probably around the one hundred mark.

Red squirrel ventures down on to the shore.
Photograph: Colin Graham

Opposite. **Sika hind emerges from the shadows. This Asian variant of the red deer was introduced to Brownsea in 1896. Some swam to the Purbeck shore where their numbers increased dramatically after the planting of conifers across the Rempstone estate in 1948-50. A few swam back to Brownsea in the 1970s to re-establish the island herd.**
Photograph: John Pitfield

This popular wisdom that the native red squirrel was ousted from most of Britain by competition from the introduced grey squirrel was analysed and rejected in volume 54 of the Journal of Ecology in 1985.

Dr J. C. Reynolds showed that in many places red squirrels died out before the grey squirrels reached their areas. In a further nine areas, where the reds were still surviving in 1982, they were coexisting with the greys.

Habitat erosion cannot be blamed. In Norfolk the extent of the red's preferred mature coniferous woodland remained roughly static but they declined nonetheless. In many other places where the red declined the available habitat was actually increasing each year.

Pox virus may have caused some of the reductions but does not invariably exterminate populations. Neither is there any evidence that the grey act as carriers for the disease. The whole question remains open.

As for Brownsea, the red squirrels share their protected environment with other much commoner mammals. Hedgehogs snuffle through the tangled undergrowth, in one of their rare traffic-free environments. Rabbits have a major warren and were probably introduced by the mediaeval monks. After this valuable supply of meat and fur had been brought to the country it was confined to cropped colonies on islands and promontories before making its general escape into the wild.

The present population of Sika deer in the Poole Basin are derived from an introduction made to Brownsea Island in 1896. The island's herd was decimated by the 1934 fire and finally became extinct during the army occupation in 1942. In the early 1970s things went full circle when Sika swam across from Goathorn and recolonised the island.

The heronry in the northern woods of Brownsea is the second largest in Britain and has more than ninety nests in most years. Throughout the breeding season and into the autumn these birds can be seen feeding on the tidal mudflats all across Poole Harbour but their numbers diminish in winter. The herons also feed in the valley of the Frome and are occasionally seen flying in from the sea at Durlston Bay. Even the bittern is sometimes seen in Dorset and two or three were found in Poole Harbour during the prolonged frosts at the start of 1963.

Brownsea is one of only three sandwich terneries on the south coast, the others being at Keyhaven and Needs Oar Point.

Most of the northern half of Brownsea is managed as a nature reserve by the Dorset Trust for Nature Conservation and visiting is restricted to small organised groups. The Trust's secretary, Miss Helen Brotherton, can see the whole north shore of the island from the windows of her house on the opposite shore at Parkstone. She, with the help of working parties of volunteers, has in many ways replaced Mrs Christie as the guardian of a unique piece of Dorset.

Warden Tony Wise shows visitors around the nature trail, the prime viewing being from a lagoon-side hide, looking across to the little bird islands with the fork-tails of the demonstrative sandwich tern, and the smaller, quieter common tern. As the young develop they are moved by their parents across to the sea wall, possibly because they feel less exposed there or for the practical reason that it is then less far for the adults to have to carry their food. Oystercatchers are the other Brownsea speciality these days, with more nesting on the island than anywhere else in Dorset or Hampshire.

BROWNSEA: DORSET'S FANTASY ISLAND

Peacock and Canada goose meet the public. Sometimes the attraction is a little too physical and the Trust has notices asking visitors to desist from plucking their feathers. In the picture below the holed and scuffed ground around the bole of the cyprus tree shows an active rabbit warren.

Photographs: Colin Graham

PINEWOOD AND REED BEDS

Typical Brownsea paths. Much of the island is wooded, with Scots pine under-stood in many parts with dense layers of rhododendron. In the northern part of the island, inside the nature reserve, there are reed beds and willow scrub.

Brownsea's lakeland is at the centre of the island, inside the restricted zone of the nature reserve.

Photographs: Colin Graham

The pines descend the cliffs to the high-water mark.

The cliff at Portland Hill, the south-east corner of Brownsea, with a raft of cormorants on what little is left of Stone Island at high water.

Closer look at the exposed sandstone cliffs, at the west end of Brownsea. The pines are never far away.

Opposite. **Brownsea Castle, under repair in 1983. The waters in the foreground are Brownsea Road, the principal anchorage in the days of sail for boats waiting the tide to go into Poole Quay.**

Opposite, bottom. **Alan Bromby attending to one of the preoccupations of wardening an island, beside the Quay boathouse in 1985.**

Re-discovery of Brownsea's Bullnose Morris, 1976

Mrs Christie's Bullnose Morris, tracked down in 1976 from Brownsea to a field in Somerset.
Photograph: Colin Groves

One of Brownsea's minor mysteries was solved in issue fifty-seven of Dorset County Magazine. The last private owner of Brownsea, Mrs Mary Florence Bonham Christie [1863-1961], had two old vehicles garaged at the island's castle. One was a Ford lorry, which was sold to the National Motor Museum and is now on show there, at Beaulieu.

The other, a Bullnose Morris, disappeared and the National Trust's guide stated its whereabouts was unknown. The magazine traced the Morris to 73 Hawkeridge Park, Westbury, in Wiltshire. In 1976 it was stripped and given a complete renovation by car enthusiast Colin Groves who is amazed at its excellent mechanical condition – "it retains the original brake linings which are still good for many more miles".

Mr Groves found the car in a field in Somerset. It seems to have been shipped from Brownsea to the mainland by Mrs Christie's grandson, John Bonham Christie, shortly after the old lady's death in 1961. He had it taken to the family estate near Frome.

Previously, the car was on Brownsea for many years and may well have come there in 1927 when Mrs Christie bought the island. What now remains to be discovered is its pre-Brownsea history.

The car was manufactured in September 1922 but carries no registration number as Brownsea was a private island and no road fund tax would have been paid. However, between 1922 and 1927 "it must have been used on public roads and had a log book", Colin Groves says.

The clue to its first years may lie in Poole. Someone locally could have sold it to Mrs Christie, or taken a photograph of it on the island during a public occasion, like the invasion of 500 jubilee scouts in 1932. At that time the registration plates may still have been in place.

These are the vehicle's specifications in case anyone has access to car documentation of the 1920s. Make: Morris Cowley, two-seater, Chassis number: D 12284. Capacity: 11.9 hp. Colour: Originally grey with black wings, but at some stage repainted blue with black wings.

Brownsea Island from the Poole side of the water, at Lilliput. The Quay and Castle complex of buildings are towards the left end. The overall view is a mass of distant pine trees. At low tide the harbour has more mud than water.
Photograph: Colin Graham

The story of the car typifies the Brownsea time warp. I am ending with a couple of pictures because any further words will be trite. It is easy to become infatuated with one of the most beautiful places on earth.

Cannon guard the Café.
Photograph: Colin Graham